Money, Money, Money,
& MUSEUMS

Money, Money, Money,
& MUSEUMS

EDITED BY TIMOTHY AMBROSE

EDINBURGH: HMSO

The Scottish Museums Council is an independent company principally funded by the Secretary of State for Scotland.

The Council's purpose is to improve the quality of local museum and gallery provision in Scotland. It provides a wide range of advice, services and financial assistance to its membership in the public and private sectors. For further details of the Council's work and a list of its publications contact:

Scottish Museums Council
County House
20-22 Torphichen Street
EDINBURGH
EH3 8JB

PREFACE

All museums need money — for displays and exhibitions, for remedial and preventive conservation, for marketing, for staffing, for equipment, for building maintenance, for training, for shop supplies, for catering supplies, for research programmes, for travel, for office supplies, for the hundred and one tasks which have to be carried out to meet the range of responsibilities which comes with running museums. This volume of papers, given at a Scottish Museums Council Conference in November 1989, investigates the ways in which museums obtain money from a plurality of sources and explores the ways in which museums spend money on meeting their responsibilities for their collections and for their users. Over the last decade, museums have been facing significant changes — changes in attitudes, changes in commitment, changes in funding patterns. Many have had to adapt and develop new approaches to financial planning in order to respond to the new decade's social, political and economic environment.

New opportunities have opened up and new skills have been called on to maximise income, both revenue and capital. New arguments have had to be deployed to potential sources of funding and with these a new professionalism has developed in income generation and fundraising. Cases for support to public and private sector sources have become more sophisticated and better argued than before. The key notes have become cost-efficiency, cost-effectiveness and value for money; museums have become more business-like.

In an increasingly competitive market-place, competition for money has become intense. Museums are having to face up to justifying their existence and arguing for and maintaining support from a wide range of sources — central and local government, trusts and sponsors, European and International organisations, patrons and individual donors.

Exploring new ways of earning money through retailing and trading, merchandising, facilities use, fees and subscriptions are all matters which the various authors here explore. Their combined experience is of enormous value in examining how museums and money relate to each other.

The Scottish Museums Council has been at the forefront of these new developments, raising new funds for its own programmes and projects, helping museums in their fund-raising endeavours and in their forward planning and disseminating information about examples of good practice in fundraising for museums of all sizes and all types. Money, Money, Money and Museums is one example of this approach to helping museums improve their financial planning.

I should like to acknowledge on behalf of the Scottish Museums Council, the support of the various contributors to this volume. I am grateful to Margaret Greeves, the Scottish Museums Council's Training Programme Co-ordinator, for organising the conference and for carrying out its detailed arrangements. Our thanks also go to Geoff Bedford, Director of HMSO Scotland, for his continued support for the Council's publications programme, and to Caroline Croyle for her design and layout of this publication. The conference on which this volume is based was generously supported by the Scottish Mutual Assurance Society.

Timothy M Ambrose
1st July 1990

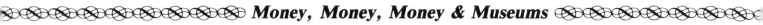
CONTENTS

INTRODUCTION

Trevor Clark, CBE, LVO, FSAScot, was Chairman of the Scottish Museums Council 1981-4, and 1987-90. He is a former overseas administrator and Trustee of the National Museums of Scotland, and is a member of the Council of the Museums Association.

I hope that readers will be forbearing for a page or two while as a layman I remind them of what Money is, however confused they may have been by chancellors, opposition Treasury spokesmen, bank governors, brokers, City yuppies, small-time politicians flogging metaphorical used cars, and sensible African market women.

Money is only a token. It lets us judge how much (for the moment) other people value one thing against another. It allows us to tuck away our reward for something we've done now and cash it in another day. And it saves us all the multilateral hassle of bartering and swapping the things we value, covet or need for survival (unless you believe that human nature will always guarantee us a free lunch).

It saves the chain of transactions involved in offering a juicy exotic mango to someone who normally helps the minister with his gardening thus giving him time to write his sermon which uplifts the morale of a taxi-driver so ensuring the continued employment of a Caribbean welder in a midlands car factory which is enabled to keep Polish steel and coal going which provides the daily bread of a union organiser whose memoirs will support a Korean word-processor manufacturer's operative who depends on an American programmer's constant revision of software demanding more powerful chips and whose

taxes pay for a marine to help to remove a freely elected dictator who contrives that a plantation manager under-rewards some under-educated guy with a cutlass who tallies his load of fruit on to a Liberian ship employing an Indonesian crew stacking containers of Hong Kong origin chilled by Swiss compressors which ensure that the cargo turns up at Felixstowe to be checked by enthusiastic customs and agricultural inspectors as fit to be supervised by paper-pushers and distributed by yet more people's brains and brawn and co-operation ultimately to a Pakistani corner grocer who sold you the mango at 11 pm because you remembered you had to bribe your neighbour's child to get up and reserve a parking place for you at half past eight. You don't have to go round the world, saying 'If I do *this* for you, will you do *that* for somebody else?' You just give him a coin to feed a meter and add a tip, which you've kept handily in your pocket. Money is a token, it is a unit of account, it is a medium of exchange, it is a store of value.

But as accumulated tokens, never forget that the sum of their value can't be greater than as a symbol of everything that is available in practical terms to exchange it for in the real world. When the price of oil trebles, when the dollar plunges, when tariff barriers crumble or are raised, the quantity of raw and manufactured materials in the world does not change one jot, the amount of brains and brawn does not alter. What people are prepared to do with them, their potential co-operation, may alter, depending on the incentives or what turns them on. The willingness to use more brains and brawn for longer hours may change, either way, the readiness to dig out more materials and turn them into something else, nourishing, useful, beautiful or gratifying, may or may not waver — the tokens will keep oscillating in relative value as judgments vary at later stages, there will be no eternal absolutes, and things may disappear or they may come forth in profusion. The human element of choice and decision comes out on top in the long run, in Tiananmen Square or King Wenceslas Square: and the tokens are always, be they bronze hoes, bags of cowrie shells or denarii, guineas or ecus, IOUs or travellers' cheques, things which are contemporaneously acceptable as mediums of exchange, of assessing bilateral value, and of storing up that value for future exchange later — or until public confidence is lost in clipped coinage, adulterated silver, or printed paper churned out without corresponding increase in purchasable resources. Once it's no longer acceptable because it looks like a confidence trick, it's worthless, as you discover when you visit any rigidly planned economy. There's infinitely more to money than Treasury grants growing on trees.

Timothy (that's the epistoller, not our editor) warns us that it is the love of money that is the root of all evil. That must put us 'museums people' in peril of our souls. All arts folk in the public sector, actually. We should never forget that of every taxpayer's pound put into public services like local government, the health service, national institutions, education, about 70 pence go straight out again into the pockets of the employees, 30 pence at the most on medicines, office stationery, objects and items, textbooks and chalk, maintenance and material support, drains and roof repairs, or whatever. Not many people want to know that, when it's a matter of what they think our national and private spending priorities are or ought to be.

But so what's new about art and money-grubbing? The Emperor Vespasian said that money had no smell, even as a tax on public lavatories. Many of our own earliest collectable works of art are coins and exotic Chinese currency like those hoes. Even if our western representational art tends not to go far beyond religious allegories on the payment of tribute money, our English playwrights taught us that money is the sinews of love, as of war; and that he that wants money, means and content is without three good friends. The Great Cham Sam himself mentioned that there are few ways in which a man can be more innocently employed than in getting money.

Virtually every justly famed musician, creator or performer, has done it for money, setting aside such as Henry VIII or Frederick the Great who had other interests. Mozart, whatever the nature of his grave, was not a pauper. You can't have forgotten the Master of Ceremonies in *Cabaret*, Joel Gray singing, 'Money Makes the World Go Round, the World Go Round. . . .' I did ask our conference organiser to consider that and other theme music for interludes in the conference which this book records, and Peter Lewis expected me to quote Abba; but I suspect that our hosts in the Royal Museum of Scotland, some of whom are opera lovers of the Rodney Milnes and Conrad Wilson kidney, refused to countenance surtitles: so I make do with English translations.

Beethoven was not thinking like Weill and Brecht when he set that bluff, sensible chap Rocco's words in *Fidelio*:

Life is nothing without money,
Anxious cares beset it round,
But when in your pockets you jingle your gold
Blind fortune you may well defy then!

Wagner was wiser than Keynes; he knew only too well what money can do, and why he needed it, and what he wouldn't do to get it, when he had Woglinde, Wellgunde and Flosshilde at the bottom of the Rhine,

8

laughing in the joyful shine of the gold, glorious beams that glitter and gleamed in the waves:

Ah how sleekly we slide in its radiance,
Come and join us, to bathe in its brightness,
Come sport and swim in its shine!

Well, you could become Master of the Universe with that gold, if you renounced carnal love. So love of that gold brought about the twilight of the gods — it was indeed the root of all evil, since mortal men then took the world over, and look at what they have done with it. It wasn't half a great work of art though.

Another great German composer, once wealthy but reduced by war to penury, was for many years anxious to see an opera take form that mixed up two Greek myths, Zeus's ravishment of Danae in the irresistible form of an ejaculation of gold coinage, and Midas's suicidal gift of touch. Richard Strauss's *Die Liebe der Danae* got as far as the dress rehearsal, but Goebbels with his impeccable good taste wouldn't let it go further because the Allied Second Front had started. *Danae's Love* begins with a chorus of creditors shouting, "Our fists are full of unpaid bills, we're coming to collect"; goes on with the heroine dreaming ecstatically of gold's glorious coolness surrounding her limbs, a radiant mantle, lovable gold; and although all ends happily in tastefully staged poverty, Midas back to being a donkey-boy and his wife Danae in designer rags, it was a hard fight against the King of the God's enticements with gold.

You cannot separate art from money, even if the inspiration comes from elsewhere. Think of the motive for Scott's Waverley novels. If you saw the Royal Museum of Scotland's magnificent display *The Wealth of a Nation*, you might well judge how little was not originally produced for hard cash. Our question in this symposium was museums and galleries that show and explain art should go to get the necessary hard cash for their salaries, buildings, displays and further scholarship. At the time we met, the English arts world and the Scottish Arts Council were congratulating the arts minister on getting a large increase to spend, which we gathered was likely to go substantially on overdue museum and gallery repairs rather than fat Italian tenors and East German stage directors; and we were waiting in Edinburgh to hear whether the Barnett formula would give us the same for Scotland, or whether it would be shifted sideways into Strathclyde motorways and saving the white elephant at Prestwick. In the event we were well rewarded by the Scottish Office. The contributions that follow show what a wide variety of opinion was assembled to share experience and wisdom as well as prejudices. They come from most varieties of the galleries and museums that most people think of when they talk about our subject. The majority tend to agree on the answer to one of the disputes of the day, but a hearing is given to the minority voice; all are thinking people who do not waste too much time wringing agonised hands, and who find solutions to their own problems. Some readers may also hear a ghostly whisper or two from the wings, wondering whether in a world of clamant individualists and prickly faiths anything is as self-evident as it is convenient to believe.

Our participants were grateful to the Scottish Mutual Assurance Society which gave generous financial support towards making this Silver Jubilee conference of the Scottish Museums Council possible. We were also grateful to the Chairman, Director and Trustees of the National Museums of Scotland for allowing us to meet on the very stage where greater glories had been promised by the Secretary of State as about to rise and bloom in the form of the long awaited dedicated Museum of Scotland. I was personally grateful to Timothy Ambrose, our Director and to Margaret Greeves, our Training Programme Co-ordinator, for organising the whole event and preparing this permanent record.

The heritage of the Future: From the British Museum's rapidly expanding print collection. Cyril E Power (1872-1951), The Tube Train, c 1934, Linocut.

WHAT DO WE NEED MONEY FOR?

Sir David M Wilson, Kt, LittD, FBA, FSA, Director of the British Museum since 1977, formerly Professor of Medieval Archaeology, University College, London. He has published numerous books and articles about Viking and Anglo-Saxon art and archaeology.

I was of course given the title of this paper. It was not one I would have wished, but I am now so fed up with the easy solutions of museums' financial problems advanced by politicians, journalists and amateurs who have little if any responsibility for museums, that I am actually going to answer the question posed by the Scottish Museums Council. Museum people are involved either in the government or in the administration of museums; why they need to be told what we need the money for is beyond me — they should know. **We need money to run museums**. I shall now proceed to explain what museums are about.

Museums are about the material they contain. The first duty of the museum curator is to look after that material, through conservation, registration and safe storage. His second duty is to make that material available to whoever wants to see it. Everything else is subordinate to those two propositions. Those who do not believe this can now leave the room.

Let us think our first unthinkable thought of the day, one of a number. Without pre-empting Mr Mason's paper can I just ask the first question of the series? Do we need museums? In one sense of the term 'need', the answer is 'no'. We can do without most things: we don't actually **need** cars, whisky and politicians, but they make life easier for us even if they are luxuries. A museum also is a bit of a luxury, but not in the sense that politicians are. We certainly don't need all the museums we have got — some are a great waste of resources, ill managed and badly run.

But museums are one of the elements in life which save us from barbarism. Not everything in life is necessarily disposable. I suppose we could melt down all the metal objects in museums, recycle the paper and canvas on which pictures are painted, use geological specimens as road metal and so on. Ideologically there have been periods, like the cultural revolution in China, when thoughts like these were expressed in action. But then, the French Revolutionaries who condemned Lavoisier to death did so with the words, 'the Republic has no need of scientists'.

Some things have to be kept. At first because they might come in useful, or because they are beautiful, or curious or even funny. Then because they have become obsolete, old, more valuable or even more curious. If objects are to be kept they must be stored and, if they are to be stored, natural curiosity insists that they should be understood. If they are to be kept for a long time they must be stored in conditions which will allow them to survive. And so a museum is created. The buzzword 'conservation' raises its ugly head. Once you have stored them you need to have store-keepers. Then people — the general public — will want to know what is stored. You then have to show the collections and then your problems start. Historians, natural scientists, archaeologists, technologists, art-historians, educators, warders, tea ladies, typists, telephonists and doormen are needed to explain the stored objects. Soon, then, you have a cash crisis because you can never pay for all the demands that are made of you. If you say that you haven't got enough money to service a museum you are given lots of advice and some sympathy. Little else.

But we still need museums because man, being above the animals, needs to know about his past and about art and nature. We cannot close them all down. So the answer to this unthinkable thought is roughly this — 'Yes we need museums, but perhaps not so many as some people think we need.' Indeed, I find it rather disheartening that people proudly boast that one museum is opened every fortnight in this country, for most of them are the products of enthusiasm which will collapse when — as inevitably — the enthusiast dies or runs out of money. We have had a number of examples of this recently — as for example the recent closures of a major collection of tobacco pipes and the Yorkshire Farming Museum. The index of the country's success in the museum world is not so much the number of museums which are opened as the support received for keeping open those that already exist. Perhaps more serious in this respect is the need to find uses for grand buildings which have lost their original function. Disused town-halls, 19th-century factories, grand houses, interesting architectural survivals, railway stations, fruit-markets and so on. We all know them — we have all seen them. If they are not made into theme parks they are thrown at museum authorities — and often in a splendid reconstructed condition. When, however, they have lost their shine, they become less attractive to visitors and, for example, become a maintenance burden on the ratepayers or on national government. The National Museums and Galleries on Merseyside for example have been half-offered the St George's Hall by Liverpool City Council, and are quite properly looking at it — but sideways with a cool and calculating eye. The British Museum will dispose of the old Senate House of London University (where its Department of Ethnography is housed) with a sigh of relief the moment space in the Bloomsbury building becomes available as the British Library moves out. Such buildings can only become museums with the promise of perpetual funding for good housekeeping. The founder of a museum has an enormous responsibility, he must think in a very long-term mode or he will pile up problems for his successors. For a museum or gallery is (as near as dammit) for ever.

Such an idea must be in the mind of all who found museums. Collectors on an ego trip should not feel that their collections can be maintained for ever without the public will to do so. A very few private museums have been privately funded in this fashion — Getty obviously springs to mind here. But who can say what the Getty money will be worth in a century's time? The Smithsonian bequest in its day approached the size of the annual budget of the United States — a lot of money 150 years ago. The Smithsonian, now the national museum of the United States, is largely funded from federal resources. John Pierpont Morgan's great library in New York — in reality a museum — is now only funded in a minor fashion from Morgan money — most comes from other sources . . . and yet Morgan was one of America's richest men when he died just before the First World War.

In this country we have at the moment a large number of independent museums — often excellently run with an emphasis on first-class preservation. But many of them survive on a hand-to-mouth basis, dependent on marketing and the cost of travel. How many of them can we afford to keep open? How many of them will survive more than 50 years without the input of public money? Even the best of them? And there is no reason why they should not receive public money: after all, landed aristocrats living in ambitious houses designed by vastly wealthy or vastly self-confident ancestors receive money from the state when their houses begin to fall about their ears: why should not museums be so funded? Of course there should be plural funding, but once a public authority sets its hand to supporting a museum it can never let up. Museums are expensive — it is cheaper to fund a swimming pool (which can after all always be closed down and the site developed) — and ultimately the major portion of a museum's support must come from the public sector. The country must decide what museums it can afford to support and give a commitment to them for ever. The others may have to go to the wall, as has recently happened at Weymouth.

In return for such support museums must be efficient and cost-effective. But it is difficult to find a scale of measurement. Is it the numbers of feet through the door? Is it the amount of money made — and, if so, is it the amount of money made through tourist revenue, or through money collected in the entrance hall, or money passed across the director's desk? Is it the scholarly output? Or can it be measured by its contribution to the educational resources of the nation or the region? What is a measurement of value to set against the enhancement by a museum of the quality of life? If it is agreed that museums form a useful public service, what value do we put on that — or have the words 'public service' lost all meaning? These questions must be answered.

Let us then look at the purpose of a museum. A museum is about objects, about their acquisition, storage, conservation and display. Museums vary in their attitude towards both acquisition and display but the centrality of curatorial and conservational functions is a sine qua non of every museum's function. To the general public, however, display predominates among the museum's functions. Hence what I call the Jorvik syndrome. Every reader will be familiar with the idea of Jorvik, even if they haven't been there. It expresses through reconstructions, models, lay figures, sound and

One of a series of gifts made by the British Museum Society. Russian Revolutionary plate 'Petrograd, Uritsky Square', 1922. After a design by Alexandra Shchekotikhina — Pototskava (1892-1967).

smells what the creators consider a small area of a Viking city looked like in the late 10th century. It also reconstructs an excavation as it is being carried out. Visitors are shown all this from the comfort of a car driven by electricity and the whole is backed by the mellifluous tones of Magnus Magnusson, who speaks a commentary which emerges from the back of one's seat. The punter is then set down in a rather conventional museum display, pusillanimously labelled as an 'artefact hall' and is quickly ushered into a shop and out onto the street having paid a rather considerable amount of money for the experience.

I am not mocking Jorvik. I am full of admiration for a professional and profitable job very well done — one done with verve and imagination. The proof of the pudding is in the eating and the takings and the visitor numbers show that it fulfils a need. But Jorvik is not a museum, it is a centre for instruction and even for entertainment. Its staff have only formal responsibility for the objects in the artefact hall, these objects belong to the Yorkshire Museum which has responsibility for them for all time. The staff of the Jorvik Centre consists basically of the technicians who refresh the display and keep alive the smells and the cars, all together with the sales staff under the supervision of a businessman/ manager. It is quite interesting that other projects mounted by roughly the same firm which produced the Jorvik Centre have not been runaway successes. These include, for example, the heritage centres at Oxford, Canterbury and Edinburgh. You will know better than why the Edinburgh centres have not been the success that they promised to be. Martin O'Halloran, in a recent number of the periodical *Leisure News*, reported that the recently opened Whisky Centre in the Old Town had halved its projected visitor numbers from

Tea ceremony in The Teahouse presented by the Urasenke Foundation as a contribution to the Japanese Galleries Appeal.

400,000 to 200,000 per annum for this year. Further, there is the problem of the projected Edinburgh Story in the Tolbooth Church next door, which was to take as its theme daily life in the 1590s as part of a £3.9 million development. Although there has been a major delay due to the unexpected bad condition of the building, Heritage Projects has decided to update the exhibition's design and are also considering other commercial uses for the building (although no details have so far been released). Why have these two projects, both basically designed by the same people that created the Jorvik Centre, not lived up to expectations? Perhaps, as O'Halloran argues, because of the increasing number of tourist attractions on the Royal Mile, but possibly also because the Vikings, who are the subject of the Jorvik Centre, had a lot of public attention focused on them (partly as the result of a major exhibition and its attendant publicity organised by the British Museum) just before the centre opened: for York, like Edinburgh, does not lack tourist attractions.

But this is only part of the story. I think that one of the real reasons that people prefer museums to centres of this sort is that generally they can have contact with the real things — objects used of the past or great works of art or of nature. Generally people wish to see the original Parthenon sculptures rather than casts. Museums which display casts and nothing else are usually pretty dreary places.

If one is to display original objects then it is clear that one must look after them and to do this the type of specialised staff I have outlined above becomes necessary. Costs rise accordingly; security becomes a greater problem, as does conservation, and we are in a spiral of cost. It is, therefore, totally unfair to compare either Jorvik, or indeed any theme park, with a museum on grounds of monetary efficiency and I get rather cross with the many businessmen who do just that. Most museums are highly efficient financially — after all we have been crawled over by financial consultants *ad nauseam* in the course of the last few years. There is,

however, no reason why the methods of display and most of the commercial practices used in such institutions should not be used in museums; indeed most of the methods used at Jorvik — even the smells — have been used at the British Museum. But the Jorvik methods are only a single part of the normal museum and in any case Joe Public would, on the whole, sooner see as many original objects as possible in the display. This again costs money as the security needed in the display of original material is very much greater than that needed when one sets out to display copies replete with smells and musak.

A museum, I must insist, is first and foremost about objects. To keep, conserve and display objects is expensive.

Let us look at one of the elements of a museum's costs that is most expensive — the staff. The British Museum — as any museum — is labour intensive. It spends more at the moment per annum on the staff and its general administrative expenses than is given to it by government in its annual grant for such purposes. Much of this expenditure goes on security. Not every museum needs the number of security staff employed by the British Museum, even in proportion to size. But the enormous value of the collections, combined with four million visitors each year, means that we have to be very careful not to open the Museum to pillagers. The Natural History Museum uses nowhere like as many security staff, for their collections are less intrinsically valuable. I should think that the number of security staff at the Jorvik Centre is very limited. It is incumbent on us, therefore, to see whether we can save on security. We have looked at economies in the field of security in some detail in the last few years. We have introduced new systems and new staffing arrangements and have indeed saved a certain amount of money. We have looked at the possibility of changing men for machines and have found that the interface with the public is essentially a human one. A man does more than a television camera — he certainly has more functions in a

The British Museum.

museum. We have also looked at the possibilities of privatising our security staff, but (as recent events in Deal have unhappily emphasised) private security is ultimately more expensive than loyal staff — and this is the professional opinion of most security advisers.

Other staff are also expensive. You don't buy professionals for nothing. And the museum must be staffed by professionals. The essential professionals include, naturally, such administrative technicians as secretaries, accountants, personnel officers, public relations experts and fundraisers. But the museum must be led by specialists in those materials which it contains; it must be led by scholars, by curators. Ultimately the objects man must control the everyday comings and goings in the museum — this has always been so and must remain so. The museum being about objects, those who understand objects must be in managerial control of the whole institution. The director must have the respect of his curatorial staff as well as of his administrative staff, ultimately the curatorial staff will

only respect another curator. Where museums have been run by administrators the result has been confusion and the break-down of communication; this was seen in the case of my own institution where an outside administrator was appointed to clear up a mess which was conceived of by the Trustees. This period of five years was arguably the most unhappy period in the life of the BM in this century. Even in the smallest museum the curator's power must be paramount. One of the unhappiest elements in the life of the provincial museum director is that he is often placed under the control of a chief officer (often the head of Leisure Services) who has no understanding of the professional status of the curator. This can and has led to some serious ethical problems which in turn have led to break-down of managerial control. Such professional services cannot be cheap, nor are the associated conservation and technical back-up which must go with it.

The staff are normally the most expensive element in the running of a museum. This is therefore one of the main reasons for our need of money.

Our next main need of money stems from the need to present the objects to the public. First of all the buildings have to be kept in good nick, and this is not always as easy as it sounds since many of the buildings are old, grand and listed. Few museums are housed in modern museum buildings — and where they are I'll bet they wish they were not. It costs the BM at the moment some £11m each year for maintenance, utilities and works and we need at least £1m more for maintenance alone, partly because the buildings have been grossly neglected by successive governments — to the extent for example that we still have a considerable amount of war damage only temporarily repaired. And the British Museum is in better shape than most museums. Further, the cost of building permanent and temporary exhibitions is horrendously expensive.

A smallish permanent gallery in the British Museum will cost half a million to refurbish with new cases, displays and lighting, whilst a special exhibition can cost at least half that sum to mount. At the moment we can fund most of these projects with help from the private sector, but I must emphasise that at the moment the British Museum is depending on the private sector for display projects which will by 1991 have cost us nearly £10m over five years. We cannot with ease go on like this, especially as only one-third of a million is coming from our building grant for this purpose. I should also say that very little of this money is coming from this country, and practically none from British industry and business. Ninety per cent of it comes from abroad. The BM has over 100 galleries. It is ridiculous to think that we can rebuild more than two galleries a year and refurbish more than six. We are thus talking in terms of half a century for the turnover of all the Museum's galleries and a refurbishment every 15 years, with a redecoration programme of each gallery with revisions every five years.

It should also be emphasised that an enormous amount of staff time goes into the display of the objects; not only of curator's time, but also of designers, technicians and conservation officers, the total on-costs of which must be in the region of 30%.

Next, museums need money to acquire objects. It is no good people saying that we don't need to collect any more objects because we have enough already. That is to display the most colossal ignorance and arrogance, as has been emphasised by the hard-headed banker who chairs the government's Reviewing Committee on the Export of Works of Art in this year's annual report. 'That,' he says, 'is like arguing that, because a hospital has a good children's ward, it is unreasonable to add an orthopaedic unit. The management of our national collections,' he goes on to say, 'cannot be static. New fields of study open up, new discoveries are made and new interests develop.' The national museums and galleries have had their purchase grants frozen since 1985, this in a period of sharply rising prices in the art world. No attempt has been made to allow these national bodies to compete in the international art market. The National Heritage Memorial Fund is now the only source to which we can turn and this is itself starved of funds and has many claims on its very limited resources. Furthermore, as the Reviewing Committee's chairman so wisely points out 'it is most undesirable that it should, in effect, have become the sole banker of last resort for any major acquisition'. Mr Scott goes on to put in a plea for a substantial increase in purchase grants, 'so that museums and galleries can buy from their own resources without needing to plead their case in competition with unspoiled coastline . . . and hibernating places for bats'. This is not to say that we must buy every Poussin that comes on the market; rather that we should, by adventurous purchases and acquisition in unfashionable areas, create the heritage of the future and not just provide an experience for the masses of today. There is more to life than bread and circuses and if taste and civilisation are to flourish in this country the public must put their money where such high ambitions can be achieved.

Collecting consists not simply in the purchase of the next Poussin offered by an impoverished nobleman. It consists of percipient acquisition by gift, by excavation, even by scavenging or by purchase, of the products of man's hands. And the people most able to do this are contained within the walls of this country's museums and galleries.

Further, it is stupid to say that, in order to acquire, a museum should sell that which it has. A museum is not a factory with raw material coming in at one end and money coming from products turned out at the other. Experience has shown that if objects are de-accessioned their disposal is frequently regretted. Most museums and galleries have sorry tales to tell about selling objects. Just one will suffice. In 1958 the Lady Lever Gallery sold a Fantin-Latour for £9,045. When it next appeared on the market a couple of years ago the Museum considered its purchase. It sold for £950,000, a multiplier of 100, and a sum which was well out of reach of the museum. I am greatly saddened to hear that another Lancashire gallery has started in a discreet fashion to sell off its collection. The BM has a very strict definition of 'duplicates' — the only objects it is allowed to sell — and in fact rarely disposes of anything of value. The idea that the various museums and galleries in the country have cellars and attics stuffed with treasures that are never consulted and simply rotting away — this idea is wrong. Much of the material is in fact the equivalent of a permanent archive, consulted rarely but of enormous value in scholarly research. Prints of historical subjects, coins of seldom investigated and long-dead kingdoms and so on. Useless to most people but to the scholar life-enhancing blood in his understanding of the history of man and his doings. Today's dimly-perceived clue is tomorrow's critical fact. The development of techniques and the increase in knowledge shed new light on material long held and cared for in museum store rooms. If we really want to raise money by the sale of objects we would have to sell our prime treasures — our Rembrandts, our de Lamerie silver or our Victoria Crosses, as the Soviet Union did in the 1930s. And think then what an outcry there would be throughout the nation and what delight in the heart of the curators of the Getty collection, what licking of lips! In fact it would make great sense if we did indeed sell our treasures because on the whole they are well-known, well-documented and much loved and a photograph will suffice. Whereas our unknown material is unloved and perhaps of greater academic potential. But even as I say this I shudder — what is made as an alleged witty throw-away remark can be taken seriously by the unreconstructed businessman. It has been reported in the press — fortunately inaccurately — that the Victoria and Albert Museum was to sell off some of its collections to improve its acquisitions. This is precisely what the good collector does, but the good museum curator should not do. The one will not live long and in any case is dealing with his private property, the other is collecting for posterity and cannot afford to make mistakes with the national heritage. The formal ethical code of museum curators, as spelt out by the Museums Association, is very clear on this point.

That there is a good deal of material in our reserve collections is a fact. Much of this material, however, cannot be shown for any length of time because of conservation conditions. Objects constructed from organic materials are particularly prone to fading and decay. Works on paper, of which the British Museum, for example, has some three million images, are particularly susceptible to deterioration if exposed to the light. Thus they are only put on display for short periods, although they are available to students who wish to see them. Much of our ethnographic collections are made of feather and wood and also have to be kept carefully away from the light and only displayed from time to time. Other material stored away consists, for example, of the detritus of human activity discovered on archaeological excavations. Such objects are of little monetary value but are an important source for the student, only fit to be kept in a museum where the context can be recorded and preserved in perpetuity so that future prehistorians can interpret them in the light of new facts.

To the really naïve the answer to all museums' problems is to charge for entry. Indeed there is an element of truth in such a statement, some of some museums' problems can indeed be resolved by charging and, whilst in principle I would like to see all museums open to the public without charge, I realise that such an ideal is unrealisable in universal terms. Certainly museums which have minor and closed collections presumably need to charge in order to have any sort of income. There is no reason not to charge for special exhibitions and special shows — although it is interesting that one of our recent exhibition sponsors at the BM (British Gas) made it a condition of sponsorship that we did not charge as they realised that many people are put off by charging for entry. Sometimes charges are ridiculously low — at the State Hermitage Museum in Leningrad a small charge is levied in order to regulate visitor flow; I believe that they still charge 10p for entry to the museum at Whitby, which in the winter months at least probably brings in all of £1 a day at most. There are

A corner of the remodelled public restaurant at the British Museum.

many and good reasons why some museums should charge, but I believe that the great national and provincial museums should not charge.

It is a canard that because museums in other countries charge, therefore we should charge. The people who parrot this are not thinking clearly. Whilst it is true that countries like France, Italy and Holland (where the British are most likely to go on holiday) do generally charge for entry, it is also true to say that the most visited museum in the world — the National Air and Space Museum in Washington — and the great museums of Berlin and Copenhagen (to name but a few) do not charge for entry. The Prado in Madrid only charges foreign nationals; but since we do not carry identity documents the British cannot go down that line. It is a proud tradition in this country that we do not charge and I hope that as many museums as possible will continue to hold fast to this wise custom.

I do not say this for sentimental reasons. The reasons are all practical. First and foremost is the fact that charges are a barrier to entry. A museum is an awesome enough thing to the unsophisticated and to erect yet another barrier against the public means that those who might well benefit most from entry might find it more difficult to come in. Charges always mean that less people come into a museum. Even the Victoria and Albert Museum's voluntary charging system introduced in 1985 had reduced attendance in the museum by 31% by 1988. The Science Museum's numbers fell by 60% in their first three months of charging. And it is perhaps better not to speak of the disastrous drop in numbers at the National Museum of Wales in the first six months after the imposition of charging, when a total of only 35,000 visitors were admitted between April and September of this year. As far as I can judge the weasel words this looks like a reduction well in excess of 60%. But enough said, it is our job to keep people coming to the country's museums, not to discourage them. I have been particularly heartened in recent weeks to read the public pronouncement of the Deputy Director of the V & A that charges, and I quote from the *Evening Standard*, 'might double our present income from donations and allow us to survive another year or so. But they won't solve our financial problems.'

The British Museum first faced up to demands for charging (and rejected them) in 1793 and one of my wisest predecessors, Sir Frederic Kenyon, fended off charges in 1929 (a fairly dicky time economically) when giving evidence before the Royal Commission on Museums and Galleries in words which are still valid today:

> The question at issue is a very simple one. Is it desired to encourage the use of the museum or not? There is not the slightest doubt that the imposition of fees discourages attendances. . . . The question, therefore, simply is whether it is worth while to exclude the public (and especially, of course, the poorer members of the public) for the sake of the pecuniary return to be expected from fees. . . . The Nation has a very large capital invested in the museum, and it is better to look for the return on it from the educational advantages offered to the public, than from the trivial taking of cash at the turnstiles.

As well as the sentiment expressed in such straight talking as this there is a further axiom to be taken into account as regards the national museums — this is that you should never trust the Treasury. Treasury is the most devious of governmental institutions in this country (and probably in all countries). What they say for this year will not necessarily apply next year. They learnt their lesson at the knee of Cardinal Morton and are quite likely to take away that which they have given you, telling you that it is not their responsibility and that you have to argue your case with the sponsor department. Although it has been agreed that we may keep all the money we earn, I am too old a bird to be taken in by such sweet talk, Treasury will soon pare away at any advantage that the museums may have won. That is their job and they are adept at doing it. So businessmen who have never had to deal with these monsters of Whitehall should listen to what is said by those who know their ways and their practices through long experience. So, although I am quite clear that I do not have the moral right to turn away from the doors of the British Museum between one and a half and two million visitors annually by charging, there are good pragmatic reasons why I should not institute proceedings which would offer such hostages to fortune. Charging as far as the British Museum is concerned is for the birds — and what is more my Trustees agree with this judgment!

Things are moving fast in this area at the moment in view of the Select Committee's recent deliberations and their report to Parliament. The evidence taken by the Committee can hardly be called balanced, and if I were not a charitable person I would suspect that they started out with the preconceived idea that museums and galleries should charge for the good of their souls, ignoring the old adage that the best things in life are free. They took evidence from only one person opposed to charging and refused to take evidence from me, although I requested a hearing; further, they refused to examine any other foreign museum than the Louvre — although it was firmly suggested to them that they go to Berlin to hear the other side of the story. I find the leaked story full of holes and hope that by the time we can all read it, it will be more balanced and less ultramontane than the press have been able to say so far. The report seems set fair to do the non-charging lobby a lot of harm if it is taken seriously. From all I hear it is a flawed document, but one which we will have to take seriously. What really worries me is the possibility that Treasury might insist that we all charge before we get a penny more.

There are serious economic arguments against charging which are too complicated to rehearse here, but I think we will have to produce them all in the next few weeks. Today I will merely stay on the high moral ground, I am myself absolutely convinced that the national museums and galleries of this country are our responsibility for all time and for the whole world and that we must not put any barrier between our collections and the public, for which they were created and who have through their taxes paid for them.

I have gone on at great length about disposal and charging because they are seen by many as panacea for all our economic ills. The arguments — or at least some of the arguments — against both these processes have been rehearsed so that the museum professional's point-of-view can be put fairly and squarely. I believe that there is unanimity among the profession about disposal policy, whilst there is a very substantial majority only against charging. I may say, however, that in all the furore of recent weeks I have had only one letter out of about 60 which opposes my views on charging.

It is also worth saying, as was emphasised by Patrick Boylan in his presidential address to the Museums Association at York, that the museum profession as a whole is pretty business-like in its financial management and control. We all run our commercial operations with energy, for here lies our folding money. There is no doubt that in the last ten years, when the ability to earn money has become not only a political ideal but an economic necessity, that we have as a profession put an enormous amount of energy into building up our commercial operations, although our buildings are in many cases difficult to adapt to such ends and our operations have often been under-capitalised (the BM started its commercial arm with a capital input of a quarter of a million pounds some 14 years ago and only ceased to rely on a bank loan about five years ago, when we were able to capitalise ourselves out of accumulated profits).

Further, museums as a whole have become pretty adept at begging. We have fought to raise money against all odds — and many of us have succeeded, though not without some strain on our livers and waistlines. The BM, if I may once again use my own museum as an example, has been raising about £3m a year in sponsorship, gifts and major donations — and this does not include the value of donations of objects to our collections. We raise some 20% of our running costs in this way. But we cannot get sponsorship money for staff (although we are able to build certain staff costs into some of our major refurbishment schemes which are privately funded). It is difficult to envisage the day when

A section of the new Japanese galleries for the construction of which over £5 million was raised in Japan and the UK.

a major public company will pay this sort of running costs or fund major unseen maintenance costs, such as rewiring or the replacement of worn out security systems or leaking roofs. And one can hardly blame them; the responsibility lies with the authority which brought the museum into being to live up to its responsibilities and keep the institution's plant and staff in good nick through proper funding.

Although much of our future lies with plural funding — or at least until the Red revolution comes — it does not seem that the nation's culture is sufficiently in tune with reality to follow the urgings of government to give

generously. Such an observation is to be seen throughout the whole world of non-social giving: universities, museums and many of the arts. Somehow it does not seem respectable in this country, as it is in the United States, to give to such non-heart-rending causes. It is going to take a long time to change thinking in such a fashion. The BM experience of fundraising has been a happy one, but by far the largest donations have come from foreign donors. A prophet is still not without honour save in his own country.

At the end of the day, however, as I said earlier on, we need money to keep the museums open. This money must come in large measure from the public sector, the private sector can and should provide the jam on the bread. Core funding is the responsibility of the nation. Our treasures are held in trust for posterity, not only for this country but for the whole world, and we must not break that trust by underfunding the warehouses which hold them. I was much heartened by the speech made by the Minister for the Arts at York in September which implies that he has taken this on board, particularly in relation to the buildings of the national museums which he wishes to see in a thoroughly refurbished state by the end of the century. All power to his elbow — I look forward to visiting London and the various other towns which are the homes of our national museums in my bath chair, clutching the Minister's speech in my gnarled and shaky hand, somewhere around 2002 (for we must allow for a certain slippage) in order to see the wondrous handiwork of the public sector and cheer, however feebly, the triumph of cultural values over Philistinism.

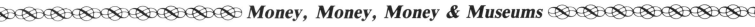

QUESTIONING
THE UNQUESTIONABLE

Douglas Mason, Parliamentary research
assistant and freelance journalist, has been an
active councillor at district and county level in
Fife. He has published a number of reports for the
Adam Smith Institute including 'Expounding the
Arts' which looked at ways of ending dependence
on state subsidies.

For a decade now, the arts in Britain have had to face serious and sustained challenges to their traditional attitudes, outlooks and ways of doing things. Principal amongst those challenges has been a consistent squeeze on the amount of public money the government was prepared to provide for their support.

Despite the recently announced increase in the money àvailable for support to the arts through the Office of Arts and Libraries any significant change in that policy seems unlikely. Indeed, the fact that the announced increase was so unexpected provides ample evidence of the atmosphere within which Britain's cultural community has had to become used to operating.

One result of that harsher economic climate has been to provoke, often for what seems to have been the first time, a serious consideration of what individual cultural organisations exist for. In the performing arts the tastes and preferences of those who attend performances, or might be persuaded to do so, have assumed increased importance over the wishes of artistic directors. The arrogant idea that art was more important than audiences has begun to give way to a welcome recognition that attracting the public is important.

Within the area of museums and what is becoming loosely called 'the heritage industry' there have been similar, if slower, moves towards recognising that attracting and interesting the public is an important activity in its own right and not to be seen just as a, sometimes irritating, adjunct to the collection and conservation of important, significant or simply interesting material.

In the museum world, however, there is not the same pressure towards a customer-related approach since in public museums, unlike in the performing arts, payment has traditionally been rare if it has existed at all.

Within the tighter financial climate it has created, the government has set out to encourage a search for alternative sources of funding, on occasion encouraging that search by the way it directs its existing financial support. The Arts Council's matching funding scheme where success in raising money from private sources is rewarded with increased government grants is an obvious example.

In the museum world it has not adopted such a clear-cut approach. It has not enforced the introduction of museum and gallery admission charges, as the government of Edward Heath set out to do in the 1970s. But its unwillingness to provide the level of financial support that museums believe they need has nonetheless created a climate within which many institutions have begun to look beyond their traditional structures towards the appointment of marketing managers and directors to exploit their collections to raise money. Museums as widely varying as the National Maritime Museum at Greenwich and the Victoria and Albert have felt it sensible to take the decision to introduce differing forms of entry charges to augment their income.

The introduction of admission charges has been very much a minority response amongst public sector museums. While private sector museums have proliferated, imposing such charges to pay their way, while exhibitions such as the 'Emperor's Warriors' and the 'Gold of the Pharaohs' have produced profits, attracting paying visitors to queue in their thousands, the traditional approach of the public museum has been to reiterate the view recently expressed in Edinburgh by Sir David Wilson, Director of the British Museum, that "Britain pioneered free entry to museums. We should not attempt to deny this great imaginative tradition."

But is it such a great imaginative tradition? It is certainly not so great a public sector tradition that it is consistently applied. Charges are imposed without complaint or protest for entry to other areas of the state heritage such as the Royal Palaces and a wide range of publicly maintained historic sites. In museums where overall entry is free there may be charges for admission to selected parts as there is for the Imax cinema within the Museum of Photography at Bradford. The same authority that enthusiastically defends its free provision of museums may, with equal enthusiasm, proclaim its success in attracting and putting on a special display for which charges are levied and from which a profit might even be made.

It is a tradition that has not prevented a public brought up in it from being attracted in large numbers to private museums, stately homes, royal palaces and other heritage establishments for all of which they seem perfectly happy to pay, sometimes quite handsomely.

Nor is it particularly imaginative. Using money taken in taxes to provide or maintain goods, services and facilities free to the public has an extremely long pedigree in the shifting history of societies and their government.

Not only, however, are public subsidies not themselves particularly imaginative they have the clear drawback of discouraging an imaginative approach amongst those who receive them. It is significant that in the first five years that National Heritage ran its 'Museum of the Year' award it was won by private museums. Even now, many years later, publicly-funded museums still share the award more or less equally with their private sector colleagues who do not share in the 'great imaginative tradition'.

Today it is still the case that, when columnists, correspondents and newspaper letter writers comment on the 'heritage industry', it is normally to compare the more welcoming atmosphere, the more convenient opening hours and the superior facilities for visitors provided by the private venue as against its public counterpart.

The reason why is not difficult to see. As John Letts, the founder of National Heritage, forcibly pointed out over a decade ago: "There is something about public fund support which sometimes appears to have the effect of extinguishing initiative and merely encouraging pointless excess." "Initiative," he said, "flourishes in independence."

I of course recognise, as some sometimes seem to forget, that what we describe as the private sector is often in receipt of some public money, either from different government sources or agencies or from other public sources such as local government.

Nonetheless, while the source of the capital funding is

important it is not the critical factor that distinguishes the private from the public sector. Where the two differ fundamentally is in the way the one depends on the state for its routine, day-to-day funding while the other relies on the payments of those who attend. If the private museum needs more money it must persuade its customers to pay more or attract more of them to attend. If the public sector museum needs more money they must persuade the politician to part with it or, more likely, convince some quango, appointed under the guise of keeping the government at arm's length from museum funding, that its needs are greater than those of other similar supplicants.

In that difference, in my view, lies the root cause for the difference of approach between museums in the public and the private sector. Those whose livelihoods depend upon attracting the paying public are likely to do more to attract and cater for that public.

Nor is that simply the view of some right-wing theorist. As Sir Roy Shaw told the House of Commons Education, Science and Arts Committee, shortly before his retirement as Director of the Victoria and Albert Museum, ". . . we have done too little asking (the public) what they want, and that does not mean going down to the lowest common denominator. We must follow the achievement of the highly successful private museums over the last few years and the whole change in presentation of historic houses."

The fact that there is such a problem is a simple consequence of the tradition of providing public museums financed wholly out of the public purse. Public museums, like so much else of public funded culture, indeed of the public sector as a whole, are dominated by the interests of the producer rather than a concern for the consumer.

What is provided, how it is provided and usually when it is provided is not done with the interests of the public in mind but usually, and understandably, with the interests of the staff and management to the fore.

It should not surprise anyone that this is so. Those who work in museums do so because of their deep personal and professional interest, often love, of the material the museum holds, not a liking for the man in the street or his money (except of course as that money may be channelled to them through taxes). Whether or not the public shares that interest is unlikely to matter too much. Indeed, for many people working on conservation or research any public interest may be seen as posing a threat, at its simplest by removing the objects of their interest for a time from the researcher's direct control and by putting them in a position where they might be subject to damage or destruction by an ignorant and uncaring general public.

One clear attraction of a policy of introducing charges for admission to museums is that it offers them some degree of independence from the bureaucratic allocation decisions of others. But the principal attraction of charges is that they create a desirable closer link with the public. Museums exist to provide a function to society and they should welcome closer links with that society and the greater effort required to make what they do attractive and understandable to its members.

And the moral principle should not be forgotten. At present, those who enjoy the benefits of museums do so, very largely, at the expense of those who do not. It may be argued, as it is with other subsidised cultural activities, that everyone pays and everyone has an equal opportunity to attend. One need only apply that argument to other areas of human activity to expose it for the nonsense it is. Should football be provided free at the taxpayers' expense? Or Soho night clubs?

But charges and ancillary income are only the icing on an increasingly dry and crumbly cake. How far governments, of either left or right, can be relied on to feed that cake in the future must be open to some doubt.

Present policiers have opened up an opportunity to seek a different kind of structure within which public museums can continue to meet their national obligations for the collection, conservation and interpretation of Britain's heritage, along with examples of the world-wide heritage within which it has to be seen and interpreted, while at the same time being under the same continuous pressure to cater for the visiting and viewing public as the private sector museum is.

One possibility which appears to me worthy of consideration would be to use the government's remaining 49% holding in British Telecom along with part of the stock in other planned privatisations and a suitable selection of gilt-edged shares to provide museums with an endowment in place of the annual grants they currently receive. They could then be placed under fully independent trusts no longer subject to the political patronage of whatever government happened to be in power.

It would then be for each institution to decide what its own future financial policy, marketing policy and admission policy would be, free of the uncertainties of government budgets.

Gold Funerary Mask of Psusennes 1. The 'Gold of the Pharaohs' exhibition generated £5.5m in the Scottish economy.

OPPORTUNITIES AND CONSTRAINTS FOR LOCAL MUSEUMS

Herbert Coutts has been Edinburgh's City Curator since 1973. He has supervised three major capital projects in the City and organised exhibitions attracting international attention. He is a former Museums Adviser to the Convention of Scottish Local Authorities.

I have been presented with something of a problem because I can't imagine anything more soporific than the title of my paper 'Opportunities and Constraints for Local Museums'. Well, for a start, I shall reverse the order and deal with the 'constraints' first and then let rip with the 'opportunities'. But I must admit that if I didn't think it would upset the Scottish Museums Council chairman, Trevor Clark, I would toss the title in the dustbin and substitute a favourite quotation from one of the sermons of the 18th century cleric Rowland Hill — 'Why should the devil have all the good tunes?' I shall use that quotation as my theme when I turn to moneymaking opportunities open to local museums.

I am the curator of a local authority museums service, and while the term 'local museums' also embraces independent, regimental and university institutions, in fact all types of museums other than the national institutions, I shall concentrate primarily on the local authority sector. Even so, much of what I have to say does have wider application.

The constraints referred to in the title of this paper are nothing more or less than the parameters, imposed and self-imposed, within which local museums operate. Inevitably, the first category we should consider are those laid upon us by legislation.

Are there any statutory restrictions to money making by local authority museums?
Given that the activity you have in mind is legal in itself (that rules out a private still in the Geological store), the answer is no. With the usual crystal clarity which our legislators employ when drafting Acts of Parliament, the present position is spelt out in the Local Government and Planning (Scotland) Act 1982. Section 15 (2) of the Act says it all: 'An islands or district council may provide or do, or arrange for the provision of or doing of, or contribute towards the expenses of providing or doing, anything necessary or expedient for the purpose of ensuring that there are available whether inside or outside their area, such facilities for recreational, sporting, cultural or social activities as they consider appropriate'. Thus the Act enables us to do 'anything necessary or expedient' to provide museum services in our areas. And in case there should be any misunderstanding as to the implications of that general power, section 16 (e) specifically authorises local authorities to 'charge for admission to any facility provided by them'. This leads me, quite naturally, on to the second category of constraints under which museums operate — policy.

Is the levying of admission charges a mortal sin?
When you confront the various options open to

museums to make money, it doesn't take a financial genius to work out that the two most effective courses of action would be to (a) levy entrance charges and (b) sell selected items from the collections. I shall deal with (b) later, but first why in the 'loadsamoney' age in which we are living have local councils so stubbornly set their faces against admission charges?

Sign at The People's Story, Edinburgh, proclaiming free admission.

As the former museums adviser to COSLA (the Convention of Scottish Local Authorities), I assisted in the drafting of its evidence to the Working Party established by the Museums and Galleries Commission, under the chairmanship of Professor John Last, to review

the role and responsibilities of local authorities in relation to museums and galleries. A section of the evidence was devoted to admission charges and trading, and this explains in simple, and straightforward, terms the thinking behind the local councils' stand. I quote: 'Scottish local authorities strongly adhere to the view that museums and galleries are, first and foremost, educational facilities. For this reason they have rejected outright the concept of charging for admission to the core collections of their institutions.'

COSLA accepts that museums which mount major, and expensive, temporary exhibitions may have to levy charges to cover their costs. It also has no worries about trading by museums, given that the publications and souvenirs available in museum shops, and the food in museum restaurants, are of good quality. If by trading, museums can reduce their running costs, this is obviously desirable. But it finished this section of the evidence by asserting: 'It is essential, however, that museums should never become profit-led, as is the case with the growing number of heritage centres which are appearing throughout the UK. It is COSLA's view that the non-profit philosophy of museums is fundamental to the high regard in which they are currently held by the public'. As a museum professional, I concur wholeheartedly with this stand, and am proud of COSLA for taking it.

So much for charges. But what about selling selected items from the collections to keep the wolf from the door? This leads us to consider the third category of constraints under which we operate — the ethical ones.

Are one-arm bandits in the orientation area and can-can girls in the sculpture court as great an ethical problem as curators think?

In these days of 'plural' funding, I suppose it is only a matter of time before some thrusting entrepreneur on a board of trustees suggests a course of action similar to that posed by my question, and in so doing reduces his director to a nervous breakdown brought on by a severe attack of ethical palpitations. Unfortunately, the likelihood that someone in authority will suggest the sale of items from the collections is no joke — it has already happened — and curators who are forced to consider this step are propelled onto an ethical minefield. The authority in question was the Audit Commission, no less, which in reporting on the shortage of display space,

The encouragement of museum visits by children and families are at the heart of the free admission policy.

inadequate storage and massive backlogs in conservation common in National Museums and Galleries in London suggested that 'vigorously pursued disposal policies' might be one way to reduce the scale of the problem. The country's museum movement is now sitting on the edge of its seat to see whether the Government will take up this idea when it frames new legislation for the London-based National Galleries — the National Gallery, the Tate Gallery and the National Portrait Gallery — perhaps giving their trustees unwanted freedom to dispose of their collections.

So what's the problem? Curators have an ethical code — a sort of Museums Association Nicene Creed — which among many provisions gives high priority to the statement: 'There must always be a strong presumption against the disposal of specimens to which a museum has assumed formal title'. This is because we believe that an object acquired by a museum, usually after much deliberation, thereafter must be held in trust for posterity. Museum collections cannot be equated to private property; they are not owned by a particular generation, but belong to all generations. A similar sentiment in favour of the long-term retention of museum collections can be found in the Museums Association's Code of Practice for Museum Authorities, which has been formally adopted by many local authorities and boards of trustees. Therefore, when the need to make money is considered by museums, selling the collections is not an option open to upright curators and honourable museum authorities.

Opportunities

We have turned our backs on the temptation to levy admission charges and our ethical code restrains us from selling the collections. What, then, can we do to attract additional resources? The first step we must take is to renounce pessimism. This is where the cleric Rowland Hill comes in. There is certainly no justification for the Beelzebub of despair monopolising all 'the good tunes' when we have a hymn book full of songs to sing to raise additional finance for our institutions. Continuing the metaphor, I suppose the first hymn to which we should give voice has to be:

'Mine eyes have seen the glory of the coming of the sponsor'.

I would be the first to admit that attracting sponsors is hard work, and that it is virtually impossible in relation

Terracotta soldiers from the 'Emperor's Warriors' exhibition which attracted substantial sponsorship from Robert Maxwell.

to the less glamorous areas of museum endeavour such as storage, security, etc. But across Scotland, there is now clear evidence that sponsors will often support temporary exhibitions, new purchases and even conservation projects. We have all attended lectures on how to attract and then retain sponsors, and so I have no intention of giving you another one. Practical experience has taught me that, above all, sponsors must be made to feel appreciated and should be given as high a profile as possible in return for their financial assistance. Often the best sponsorship results come from

companies with whom a long-term relationship has been built. To quote just one example, ten years ago Edinburgh City Museums and Galleries first established contact with the insurance giant, the Life Association of Scotland Group over a small amount of sponsorship, literally a few hundred pounds, given to a doll exhibition. In 1985 the LAS Group sponsored the education pack for 'The Emperor's Warriors' exhibition, which involved more money than the first project, a few thousand pounds, but it was still a relatively small sum. The main sponsor of the exhibition was Robert

Maxwell, the newspaper proprietor, to the tune of a guarantee against loss of £60,000. Last year we had no further to go than the LAS Group when we were in search of a main sponsor for 'Gold of the Pharaohs'. On that occasion they agreed sponsorship to the tune of £110,000, £30,000 of which was made available immediately towards the cost of mounting the exhibition, the balance, £80,000, being a guarantee against loss. The guarantee was never called upon as the exhibition made a profit of £150,000.

As a last word on this topic, I would urge you not to scorn sponsorship in kind. Many concerns are not able to give money but if asked will provide practical assistance without charge. We have received this sort of valuable sponsorship from concerns ranging from British Airways to a packaging firm and from Radio Forth to British Telecom. This sort of sponsorship is as important as a cheque and certainly merits the same level of public acknowledgement.

Don't expect any help from the Government!

Since Noah was a boy it has been fashionable to condemn the Government, all Governments, for adopting a penny-pinching attitude towards the needs of museums. Certainly, our present rulers have not covered themselves with glory over their failure in recent years to vote the national museums and galleries sufficient funds to meet their day-to-day running costs. But even the harshest of the Government's critics had to welcome the announcement by the Minister for the Arts of a bigger than expected rise in funding for the arts over the next two years, included among which was a major boost in the building and maintenance programmes of the national museums and galleries. While it remains the long-term aim of the Government to reduce the level of its direct funding and encourage the growth of sponsorship, there is still a great deal of financial help to be obtained from Government agencies, given that you fill up the relevant forms, usually in triplicate, and ask politely. Indeed, the problem for the Curator of a local museum is that assistance is available from such a

Nineteenth-century banner conserved with grant-aid from the Scottish Museums Council.

perplexingly diverse range of bodies. The trick is to match the project which you have in mind with the correct grant-aid source.

Of course, readers will be aware of the schemes operated by the Scottish Museums Council. Then there is the help which can be obtained from the Scottish Arts Council, including grants towards staging temporary fine art exhibitions, establishing artists-in-residence posts, commissioning new works of art, and even, from the housing the arts fund, grants towards building projects.

Institutions wishing to add to their collections can benefit from the Local Museums Purchase Fund, administered by the National Museums. To the considerable anxiety of museum curators, the Government has not increased the value of the Scottish Fund in recent years, but the money that is available should be exploited to the full. Only in this way can we hope to persuade the Government that it is not enough.

If your museum, or country house, is located in extensive grounds there is a chance that you might be eligible for assistance from the Countryside Commission, towards the cost of providing improved parking, seating and picnic areas and even toilets for visitors — as we managed to attract for Lauriston Castle, despite the fact that it is located within the city boundaries. Should you wish to commission a new work of craftsmanship, useful advice and part-funding is available from the Crafts Division of the Scottish Development Agency. But for the biggest bucks of all, the ones that you need if you are planning a major building, extension or conversion project, you need to turn to the Highlands and Islands Development Board, the Scottish Development Agency or the Scottish Tourist Board. In 1986 we received £132,000 from the STB towards the opening of an extension to the Museum of Childhood, the total cost of which was £854,000. If your museum is located in an area of great deprivation, funds may also be available to you from the European Commission. There are even more sources of Government help which I don't have time to mention. From this brief *tour de l'horizon* you will see that despite all the monetarist propaganda, Government agencies are assisting museums on a considerable scale. (Perhaps we shouldn't give the game away by talking too loudly about it!) As I see it, it is the duty of every curator of a local museum to make full use of such help as long as it is available.

Self-help

In reviewing the money-making opportunities available to museums, having dealt with sponsorship and Government assistance, we should now turn to 'self-help'. I would include under this heading shops, restaurants, donations boxes, gallery hires, reproduction charges and facility fees.

Can any money be made from museum shops or are they just loss-making temples to curatorial egotism?

Up until a few years ago most shops in Scottish museums and galleries were little more than a joke. More often than not, they consisted of a primitive sales desk, stocked with off-printed papers from academic journals and a few dreary postcards. And, naturally, the member of staff selected to represent the smiling face of the museum behind the sales desk generally fell into the dragon at the door category. But everything is much better now, isn't it?

Certainly, today's museum shops look more welcoming, though most of them, and I include my own in this criticism, still tend to be too small. There is, I understand, an old maxim in the retail trade — 'you sell what you show'. For this you need a well-lit, comfortable space where visitors can linger and browse without falling over each other. The shop should be easy to find and whenever possible should be located close to the museum's entrance/exit. Many visitors leave the exploration of the shop to the end of the day, and so if it is the practice in your museum to close the shop 30 minutes before the rest of the building to clear the tills, etc, you could be losing many thousand of pounds of potential sales in a year.

Decisions as to the sort of stock to carry can be the cause of bitter conflict between shop managers and curators. The manager is generally under instructions to maximise profit, by stocking a range of publications and other goods that offers something for all pockets and is loosely relevant to the institution's role and collections. Curators, on the other hand, tend to view the purpose of the shop from the other end of the telescope, stressing the importance of meeting the needs of

The City of Edinburgh Art Centre café which earns useful income and is a magnet to visitors.

scholarship and insisting that it carry publications which are so specialist in their nature there is no likelihood of their selling in any quantity. I have been as guilty as the next curator over bringing into being catalogues that should never have been published and have subsequently been piled high in the stock room. Curatorial vanity needs to be constantly guarded against and we should listen more closely to the commercial advice offered by our shop managers and be less worried about offending our friends by refusing to stock their boring books.

On the other hand, if you are confident that the exhibition you are planning is going to be a blockbuster, which will attract several hundred thousand visitors, there's a lot to be said for taking your courage in both hands. To maximise the income-making potential of such a show, a large exhibition shop is essential. In addition to the usual souvenirs which any event of this scale spawns (mugs, t-shirts, badges, pencils, etc), an attractive range of publications is merited. You may be interested to learn the unit costs and retail prices of the 'Gold of the Pharaohs' publications. The catalogue cost £1.85 to publish and sold for £4.85, the education pack cost £1.33 and retailed at £2.90, the children's book cost 35p and sold at £1.95 and the wall chart was published for 75p and retailed at £2. These publications were reprinted several times during the exhibition's 14-week run and made a significant contribution to the shop's turnover of £454,673.[1] But please remember that blockbuster shows are rare and, from the commercial point of view, most exhibition catalogues should never be published.

Never mind about the salmonella, what about the profits?

Studies of the spending patterns of tourists have shown that a significant element of their daily spend is on food. Hardly surprising. But what is surprising, if not shocking, is that many museums in Scotland still do not have a tea room or cafe in which visitors can obtain physical sustenance in between bouts of educational and spiritual uplift. By providing appetising and wholesome meals and snacks, a museum cafe can generate useful income and serve as a magnet to visitors in its own right. Also, when setting up your cafe, don't forget to obtain a refreshments licence. Some years ago, Sir Roy Strong, the former Director of the Victoria and Albert Museum, in a memorable phrase stressed the importance of 'martinis with the Bellinis'. Wine with your meal is a part of civilised living and should be as easily available in a museum cafe as it is in a High Street restaurant. And in any case it increases the income.

Donations boxes

One source of income we should not despise is the humble donations box. I am not suggesting that you should solicit donations in the sort of heavy-handed way which was attempted at the Victoria and Albert Museum. But an attractive-looking donations box placed near the entrance/exit, accompanied by a simple caption explaining that the proceeds will be used for the benefit of the museum, can generate useful income. Our experience is that most visitors make donations on their way out. Some museums suggest the level of donations expected. We have not done this because we have no wish to embarrass the poor.

Why shouldn't wedding receptions be held in the dinosaur hall?

I like to think of myself as unstuffy but I have severe reservations about the recent phenomenon of wedding receptions and, by all accounts fairly wild parties, among the dinosaurs at the Natural History Museum in London. It has been reported that the normal ban on smoking has been waived for such events, which can continue until 4 am. However, I wish to emphasise that I am not in principle against the marketing of museums and galleries as hugely attractive locations for private receptions, product launches, etc. In my view, there is substantial income to be made from this source. But it is essential that the collections are protected, the non-smoking rule is applied as normal and museums do not distort their main educational role in pursuit of this sort of business. To return to 'Gold of the Pharaohs', we made the exhibition available for 'exclusive' viewings to hotels, a wide range of businesses, and even some charitable organisations for £1,000 per evening. Everything was handled decorously, there were no riots among the mummies, and at the close of the exhibition we were £35,000 better off as a result of this particular initiative.

Paying for the image

I have long held the view that museums and galleries consistently fail to exploit to the full the income earning capacity of copyright and reproduction fees in relation to works in their ownership. The reproduction fees charged by The Bridgeman Art Library are something of an eye-opener. Too often local museums virtually give away to publishers the right to use images from the collections for a laughably low fee (if any) and a standard acknowledgement. I suspect that all of us need to review the reproduction charges we levy. Also, a deal with a London-based commercial art library such as Bridgeman is worth considering. It means that images from your collection will be easily accessible to the picture researchers employed by the major card and calendar publishers, who pay high prices for the right to reproduce good quality fine and decorative arts material. Such libraries pay the museum or gallery owning the work an agency fee each time it is reproduced.

A cognate matter is the question of the facility fee we generally forget to charge when a TV company asks to use our local museum as a backcloth for one of its latest epics. The standard undertaking is that the filming will be over in 30 minutes, but generally it occupies two days. There are usually promises of a handsome acknowledgement when the epic is transmitted three years hence but unfortunately these are not always honoured. Before agreeing to filming you should calculate the cost of the disruption generated by the presence of the TV crew, add 100%, and insist on a written undertaking that a facility fee of that order will be paid. All major television companies make an allowance for facility fees in their budgets for dramas and documentaries. When asked (they never offer) it is my experience that they generally pay up without protest.

Invisible earnings

When I was less than half my present age, financial journalists used to become greatly worried by the balance of trade deficit between imported and exported manufactured goods. Then one day some bright economist tripped over a great pile of invisible earnings (the banking and insurance services that Britain was providing for most of the world) and when the value of these was added to the balance of trade equation the deficit turned into a surplus and everyone was happy. Something similar has happened in the world of museums recently and it would be remiss of me to end this talk without mentioning it. John Myerscough in the Policy Studies Institute's report 'The Economic Importance of the Arts'[2] demonstrated that museums can make a significant contribution to the economies of the localities in which they are set, by providing direct (and indirect) employment and by attracting tourist spending. In Edinburgh these findings have been confirmed by an economic impact survey which we commissioned in connection with the 'Gold of the Pharaohs' exhibition. This indicated that the show generated £5.5m of expenditure in the Scottish economy, £4.4m of which was in the capital city.[3] Thus, it has been convincingly demonstrated that museums by their very existence, as well as fulfilling a vital educational role, actually give economic sustenance to the area they serve.

Conclusion

To sum up, I believe it to be the duty of those in power in local government to honour the inheritance of their predecessors and properly fund the museums and galleries in their care. But equally it is incumbent upon the curators administering local museums to assist the authorities they serve by doing all that they can to reduce the net running costs of their institutions. The opportunities are all around us. We must go out and seize them.

Bibliography

[1] Coutts, H (1988) 'Scotland's first £1m Blockbuster', *Scottish Museum News*, Winter issue, pp 10-15.

[2] Myerscough, J et al (1988) *The Economic Importance of the Arts in Britain*, Policy Studies Institute.

[3] Coutts, H and Woodward, S (1989) 'The Midas Touch: The economic impact of Gold of the Pharaohs', *Museums Journal*, June issue, pp 25-27.

Artist's impression of town street, Beamish.

DEPENDENCE OR INDEPENDENCE

Peter Lewis is Director of the North of England Open Air Museum, Beamish, which was European Museum of the Year in 1987. He was the Piermaster at the award-winning Wigan Pier development until taking up his appointment at Beamish.

The title of this publication MONEY MONEY MONEY suggests a flood of finance; a positive superfluity of cash; what my teenage son refers to as ready dosh. I am not equipped to write on such a state of riches. I can only write of Museums and money with that last word very much in small print.

I presently have the honour to be the Director of Beamish, The North of England Open Air Museum, just south of the well guarded border. It is a rarity in that it is neither national nor local but is a regional museum. Unlike Ulster, for example, it receives no government funding. Its trustees are from local government representing the counties of Northumberland, Durham and Cleveland, the cities of Newcastle upon Tyne, Sunderland and Gateshead and the boroughs of South and North Tyneside. Frank Atkinson, my predecessor, started collecting for a museum of northern life in the late 'fifties, obtained a site in 1970 and opened exhibitions first in Beamish Hall and then in the open air of Beamish Valley. By the time he left in 1987 the museum had been designated British Museum of the Year, European Museum of the Year and was one of the few museums categorised by Kenneth Hudson as worldwide 'Museums of Influence'. These awards and accolades earned a multitude of visitors and many friends but possibly confirmed in the minds of some

curators their worst fears about open air museums. Fallaciously, but all too often, popularity is assumed to be synonymous with poor standards.

I was asked to sketch briefly the way in which my museum is funded and to comment upon both its success and its problems. Rather than a general paper this is a **particular** one. Beamish is presented to you not as a blueprint but as a case study. If you retain nothing but proof of your fears about charging in museums then this exercise will have been worthwhile. It may also confirm your worst apprehensions on the appointment of museum directors.

First, quickly, let me illustrate what the Museum is. It occupies a site of 300 acres in the Durham countryside with little or no access by public transport. Its size, larger than most town or city centres, is such that when you stand in the centre of the valley bowl the Museum stretches to the horizon and beyond. Within that valley we have started, and have perhaps 10% completed, the recreation of life of the North East of England in the first decades of this century. Some buildings on site we have inherited. Most are simple vernacular buildings which we have 'deconstructed' and moved from locations in the region and furnished from our very extensive collections of artefacts. We seek, by the

A view of the town street, Beamish.

around the site. They discover a section of a town street that contains a park and bandstand. At weekends bands play. Three shops from the Annfield Plain Co-operative Society, grocery, drapery and hardware, are open for inspection and peopled, as elsewhere on site, by demonstrators in period costume. Our smells are authentic, coffee beans, lavender, tarred rope, turpentine. We don't use aerosols. The sounds too are real, coffee grinding, gramophones, the noise overhead of the first Lamson Paragon cash system. Visitors constantly offer their Co-op Dividend numbers and those of their mothers and grandmothers. Across the street is a typical stationer and printer. The presses work. There is a smell of ink. The Sun Inn is open. You can drink here and visit the four brewery dray horses in the back stables where again the smells are totally authentic. In a row of six mid-19th-century houses, rescued from Gateshead's Ravensworth Terrace we have recreated the house of a piano and elocution teacher, a dentist's surgery and residence, a solicitor's office. Not only the public rooms but the kitchens, bathrooms and bedrooms are open to view and are peopled. A short walk takes visitors to the Station Yard. Built at Rowley, once a halt in the hills above Consett, the station boasted neither gas nor electricity but was lit by oil. The wrought iron bridge was collected from Crook, the signal box from Carrs Hill East, the coal merchants' office from Hexham. Together with other buildings from the region they illustrate the local importance of the North Eastern Railway Company. We try to keep locomotives in steam though there are more often goods vehicles than passenger trains. We would like to do more. But here is a clear illustration of financial problems. Visitors delight in both trams and trains, but trams offer, not only historical insights, but the ability to move people more effectively. Consequently the greater part of our resources are invested in those trams we presently run, in their maintenance and in the restoration of the four other trams we so obviously need.

cottages, houses, shops, mines, farms, etc, to show, in part, people's lives, their pastimes and occupations. The scale is both large and intimate. The Museum is large but the detail is precise, even pernickety. We do not pretend that it is yet comprehensive. We do not cover all societies or classes but we are moving slowly towards that unreachable aim and are endeavouring to harden the image, to sharpen our interpretation, to provoke those who use the museum.

Visitors who come on site find a large car park and working period trams or a replica bus to transport them

Home Farm we discovered on site and have restored to a working period farm. It's the home base of our

A traditional farmhouse at Home Farm, Beamish.

animals, of our herd of Durham Shorthorn cattle, descendants of the Durham ox, of Saddleback pigs, Teeswater sheep and flocks of hens, bantams, ducks, geese and turkeys. They live in the barns and fields of the Museum. They were once common breeds. Soon they will be rare, not least the shorthorns whose semen and foetuses we keep for safety in deep freeze. For some visitors the Farm evokes no more than the warm domesticity of the Farmhouse where we bake bread and scones, launder and make mats. For others it's a welcome place to sit down after long walking. We do try to counter this cosy 'Janet and John' image of farming, to remind visitors that a farm is not a children's zoo

compound but a food factory. So we do shear sheep, pluck poultry, hold leek shows, work the smithy and, new for this year, produce Beamish cheese in our dairy. You can't, given modern susceptibilities, show everything. The castration of lambs or the slaughter of pigs would obviously be unacceptable as is the treatment of sick animals. We keep separate quarters for animals that are off colour.

In the colliery area we have the heapstead from Gateshead and the tall stone engine house with its 1855 Joicey Steam Winder from the Beamish 2nd Pit at Chophill. This is the only survivor of this type of vertical steam winding engine once so common in the Northern coalfields. Close by is Mahogany Drift, a mine here long before the Museum. Visitors can walk underground into 'G' seam to experience the working conditions of miners. Adjacent to the flat-topped pit heap is a row of pit cottages from Francis Street, Hetton le Hole near Sunderland. One cottage is laid out as a colliery office. The others show how colliers lived, complete with back netties and communal bread ovens. We are sometimes accused by journalists and academics, from what I've come to call 'The Hewison Industry', of showing too rosy a view of mining life, of romancing the grime. They insist that the rooms of colliers' cottages were never this big nor so well furnished. They are wrong. They have fallen prey to the many temptations of wishing the past blacker than it sometimes was. They forget that colliers and their wives did buy solid furniture when they set up home and endeavoured to provide warmth and good food for their families. As someone, who for six months, lived on site in No. 6 Francis Street, I can confirm that the cottage was cosy

— but far from rosy. I have never been a boy scout but I quickly learned to keep in a fire for days on end. I also battled against the unbeatable coatings of dust on every surface. When there were merely two of us 'the living was easy'. When the four of us in the family were reunited we fought our individual untidinesses and the total lack of privacy. These long back gardens with their root crops and poultry were not there for provender alone. They were valuable escapes from the pressures of perhaps eight people or more living in a two-up-two-down cottage.

The Museum is not complete. We have ambitious plans to rescue other buildings. In 1990 we plan to take back into the Museum a second farm, set high on the hill at Pockerley, complete with its own pele tower, proof of the past depredations of the Scots. In the colliery village the reconstruction of Beamish Wesleyan Methodist Chapel is nearly complete and the foundations are being laid of the old Victorian Board School from East Stanley. Our tram track will, in the next few years, complete the loop around the site and the town street will grow with a sweet factory, garage, chemist's shop, pawnbrokers and covered glass arcade. My private dream is to find a small civic building to house an Edwardian museum and gallery. There exists too an overwhelming need to build a home in the middle of the site for our archives and photographic collections. These need to be made more accessible. Development cannot all be in buildings and artefacts, however. The craftsmen and demonstrators who people our houses and shops have the most difficult task of anybody who works in Beamish. Anybody who works or dabbles in 'living history' knows the temptations of inaccurate interpretation, of over-theatricality to please visitors. Boredom sets in when the Museum is quiet, panic when it's busy. We have this year made a new curatorial appointment, a Keeper of Interpretation. He has solid experience as a 'museum professional' but his task is to work alongside the other keepers to ensure the accuracy and the excellence of our demonstrators. Together with his supervisors, he is responsible for the quality of the public performance at

Bread being baked in a coal-fired oven in the pit cottages in the Colliery village at Beamish.

all times when the Museum is open and we're having to organise crash training courses for our staff, both permanent and seasonal. It all costs energy, enthusiasm and ultimately — money — money and yet more money.

So how is such a museum funded? What are the revenue costs? We receive each year a grant, paid per capita, from our eight local authorities. This year it represents approximately one third of a million pounds. In the early days the museum grant represented nearly two thirds of our needs. Next year the grant will cover approximately 14% of the revenue budget. The pattern of funding has changed and is changing still. Although a local authority museum, we are forced more and more to behave as an independent one. We are thus heavily dependent not only on a regular flow of visitors but a regularly **growing** flow of visitors. Such is the balance between dependence and independence.

From virtually its earliest days the Museum has been obliged to charge for admission. Those trustees, who provided and still provide free museums in their own localities, insisted on charges at Beamish which were once a few pence and are now several pounds. As a cockney working-class boy much of my primary and secondary school education was polished by free access to London's great galleries and museums. I would like to see free admission at Beamish. To achieve this I would need grants of over £2.5 million in the coming year. I am sensible enough to realise that this is not politically a practicality.

The Museum attracts visitors both local and from further afield. The growth has not been constant. In the early '80s the museum suffered, through lack of development and the international oil crisis, a severe drop in visitor levels and shortfalls in money. Subsequently, visitor figures have improved and have reached half a million a year but all who lived through the trough of poor attendance recall it nostalgically. I use the word **nostalgically** deliberately. Like **heritage** it's a word that has been 'rubbished' by Hewison et al.

It means literally **remembrance with pain**. That's a precise phrase, one that shouldn't be lost. I apologise for the linguistic digression.

I have chosen to show a simplified version of revenue costs going back to 1979, then to 1984 and in 1989 — a snapshot of ten and five years ago. In each of these years the Museum had a small revenue surplus or deficit but the figures are usefully comparable.

Although our grant increases it does not do so at a scale that matches either inflation or need. In real terms the grant was worth more in the late '70s than in the late '80s. As a result we have become heavily dependent on admissions, retailing and catering. You can see the scale of their growth. I am only sufficiently numerate to pray that the growth necessary to break even is arithmetic and not geometric. The increase in turnover has been high but so have costs and I can only hope that profits are maintained. As some readers will be aware, not all museum shops and cafeterias make a profit. Not all directorial entrepreneurial activity is productive. Looking at my fellow museum directors I sometimes note with

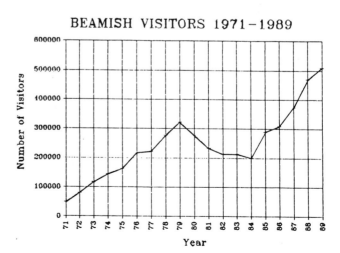

BEAMISH VISITORS 1971–1989

Visitors to Beamish, 1971-1989.

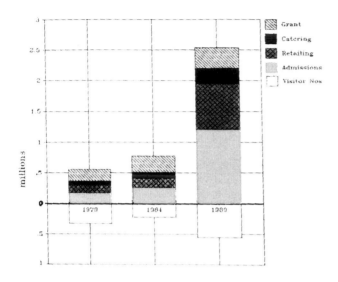

Income sources for selected years at Beamish.

amusement or bemusement the risks they take. The most dedicated of curators can become obsessed by business, making deals, and launching into retailing. We all know of the ex-director of a national museum who sought to make it like Laura Ashley. Last year I heard another director of a regional museum, laud his latest activity. He wished, he said, to become the George Davis of the museum world. Whatever next? I rest my case but do acknowledge that my initial task at Beamish was not to strengthen the marketing and retailing divisions but to point to shortfalls in curatorial provision and, hopefully, to cure them. Returning to the charts, the greatest rise in costs over the decade has been in people, from roughly a quarter of a million pounds, to double that in 1984, to a figure well in excess of a million pounds now. We presently employ nearly two hundred permanent and seasonal staff each year. We've created jobs, however inadequately paid, in an area of very high unemployment. The Government gives us no credit either financial or moral. Indeed hidden in those figures are large payments to the Government in Value

Added Tax. Ten years ago, after reclaiming some VAT, we paid £48,000 to the Treasury. This year that figure will be approximately a quarter of a million pounds. Next year the repayment will be greater than the amount we receive in grant. If the government is seeking a way to help arts organisations, museums and galleries, the reduction or zero-rating of value added tax is a solution. I don't believe that the European Commission would be allowed to stand in the way of this approach if Downing Street, Numbers 10 and 11, made it clear that this was **paramount**. Given growth in employment in Beamish and the surrounding area, the Government have had a good deal. The Economics Department of the University of Durham is presently doing a detailed analysis of the economic and social impact of Beamish on the North East. Funded by the Rowntree Memorial Trust, the report comes out in 1990. My own reading of the initial figures suggest that merely in the employment field the value to the Exchequer, in saved benefits alone, will be over a million pounds. So much for whingeing museum directors who demand public funds, or institutions which are described as black, bottomless pits into which the taxpayer pours money!

Where else does a museum like Beamish look for its finance? First to Europe. Our next six year plan will hopefully be assisted by the EEC, who have indicated privately but not yet in writing, that they will fund half of the £3.5 million to finance the development programme. We must match those funds from local authorities, from the Museum's own hoped-for revenue surpluses and from the Beamish Development Trust, a separate charitable trust, with its own Director. He seeks to persuade the great and the good of the North East to part with gifts, covenants and sponsorship. Some museums are good at this. The Natural History Museum has recently announced a £1 million green grant from Shell. The Science Museum has persuaded Sainsburys and others to support food and farming exhibitions. Regionally, Ironbridge, has a record, over many years, of raising substantial amounts of money. Beamish has not. This may well be due to a deficiency of tactics or a lack of hard-sell. It is mainly caused, however, by the lack of major industrial or commercial companies in the North East. Our largest companies have their Head Offices elsewhere in Britian or abroad. But then all companies in Britain are deluged with requests from the arts, museums, hospitals, charity foundations and individuals. The Managing Director of one small local company tells me that three years ago he received two begging letters a month. He now averages more than 250.

There is some evidence nationally of company charity fatigue. The recently published report of the Charity Arts Foundation says that business donations have decreased from 0.21% of pre-tax profits to 0.18%. Only 30 members of the Per Cent Club, companies committed to give 1%, do so. Only 63 companies give more than 0.5%. Michael Brophy, the Foundation's Director, attributed this decline to a growing belief that the Government was not pulling its weight and that at least a 20% increase in Government contribution is needed to restore private confidence. Colin Tweedy, the Director of ABSA, the Association for Business Sponsorship of the Arts, has warned that 'in the old days sponsorship was some of the icing on the cake. Nowadays it is expected to be the flour, the butter and the raisins too'. More ominously the Chairman of the Royal Exchange Insurance Company who gave £1.5 million to the Royal Shakespeare Company, warned that repeat donations were in jeopardy because his company felt that their money had been used to fill deficiencies in Government funding rather than providing additional support to the RSC. Recent announcements of extra funds from the Arts Minister to the Arts Council do very little to change this situation. I'll return to these later.

Without gifts many museums are resorting to sponsorship, to lettings of their spaces. In London, I heard a senior manager of the National History Museum explain that corporate hospitality would bring in a quarter of a million pounds this year, perhaps £450,000 next year, to his museum. I am not against the principle but I was shocked by much of the practice. He did

admit that priority in galleries was sometimes given to caterers rather than visitors, a situation that has also occurred in the National Railway Museum and elsewhere. I was also intrigued to learn from the Natural History Museum that they insist that the identities of companies using the museum are never published, either by the museum or the company, in case of adverse publicity or possible demonstrations. This secrecy over access, the lack of openness, is frightening. I have to say that we do allow television filming and a small amount of corporate hospitality at Beamish. The firm and mandatory rule is that this occurs only before and after hours. A single visitor in the Museum is entitled to total access no matter the scale of entrepreneurial profits. I have also detected the strain that overtime or evening working places upon staff in all disciplines and at all levels. You can't manage evening activities with your daytime staff. However clean the museum the following day, there is often a tiredness or lack of energy that is difficult to correct.

There has been much discussion in recent years of the need for proper marketing in museums — is it to be the means or the master of the mission? Peter Ames of the Boston Museum of Science in association with British and American museum colleagues makes the point that, as museums mature, they are pressurised to reconsider their missions. Sponsorship provides as much tension as support for the mission. This is not merely the ethical question of accepting exhibition sponsorship from British Nuclear Fuels or the possibility, for example, as yet totally hypothetical, of Nissan offering large quantities of Yen to advertise their latest cars on a Beamish period tram. It takes more subtle forms.

A mission-driven museum plan studies the desires and interests of present and future visitors, but is based on the concerns of future generations and what the museum believes present visitors **need** or should know. A market driven museum focuses on what the contemporary market **wants** and what it thinks it needs. This difference between **wants** and **needs** is important. I try to give visitors what they need. Although I am aware that this is ideologically unsound, possibly elitist, it is nevertheless culturally more creative. The market and the mission both have common elements but there **are** clashes. A market-orientated exhibition may — and I only say may — be more concerned with attracting an audience than with the quality of the message or the dignity of the objects. To balance the two is a constant challenge. A typical symptom of the tension is an emphasis on the pace and size of temporary exhibitions. In an open air museum there is a constant need for new things, for more to see. A larger percentage of space is created for ancillary services and a consequent squeeze occurs on exhibition and gallery space. Large increases in attendance can strain physical capacity, but we have to learn to manage success, to cope with large growths in income from restaurants, shops and space rentals. All of these should lead to greater vitality, visibility and, hopefully, economic health. But extensive publicity or advertising can erode a museum's integrity. This is no place to comment on a recent well recorded campaign but it does seem to me that even high increases in attendances did not justify the vulgarisation of the Victoria and Albert Museum. The balance between **earning** and **learning** was lost. The advertising was successful in the short term but ultimately is not sensible. This was a text book case proving that what is often good publicity can be the poorest of poor marketing.

The only safeguard to these dangers is curatorial conscience and directorial oversight. These are not always compatible — even or especially at Beamish. If a museum is to be true to its mission it does have to know what it **is**. One of the benefits of compulsory registration, of which we in the North East have had the first experience, has been to expose the lack of real mission statements in most museums, and the outdated and dusty nature of many others. Beamish was no exception to this. We had a set of pious phrases, a general statement of our hopes and aspirations and we have had to sharpen it. Our long-term aims were stated but their mid-term application has to be assessed at least twice a year. It's our only defence against decay of principles. It is not easy to monitor — there is a constant clash between curatorial and marketing staff. Most of the time, the tension is creative rather than self-destructive. I firmly believe that the conscience of the Museum has to reside in its junior and middle management staff. For example at our regular curatorial meetings, regrettably only held six times a year, there is freedom of expression. Neither I, nor my Deputy Director, chair the meeting. That is done by the Senior Keeper. Keepers, Assistant Keepers, Researchers, Librarians and Technicians are allowed to speak without penalty. It should be written into their job descriptions. This is not a licence for bloody-mindedness but a necessary expression of conscience, of involvement with policy. They don't always win but they do sometimes. Eloquence, however junior, has sometimes stopped this particular oil tanker in mid-channel and caused a change of speed or direction.

I return, however, to the simple text of this sermon. Museums, like man, cannot live on bread alone, but they certainly can't exist without it. Whatever criticisms are levelled at museums and galleries, unless our work is internally more effective and externally better funded, there will not be a heritage, nor even a **heritage industry**, for us and others to be critical about. Museums and galleries are not, despite assurances to the contrary, well regarded by authority. We do occasionally receive compliments:

Museums are dynamic, forward thinking institutions . . . they exhibit imagination, innovation and vigour — they represent an outstanding and overall contribution to our national life.

Later in the year the following words were reported:

This should have been called an Exhibition Centre and not a museum — a museum is something dusty and dead.

Artist's impression of town street, Beamish.

The speaker in each case (and I am indebted to a correspondent in the *Museums Journal* for having highlighted them) was the Right Honourable Margaret Thatcher MP and they exemplify the double standards that exist in Government. Advisers advise, ministers decide and the Prime Minister derides! Whitehall and Westminster often speak with forked tongues.

Why don't they like us more? Why this ambivalence? How has this distrust built up? We who labour in museums are most at fault. I have worked in a variety of professions. I know of no other so fractured, so splenetic, so unsupportive in its attitudes to colleagues. We behave like colonies of robins who sing only to frighten off the other robins. We're afraid of birdsong in unison. Rarely do we support the Museums Association but then rarely does it deserve our support. We as members have little confidence in its style of management or its efficiency. It is poor at speaking **for** us and hardly speaks **to** us at all. Over the past two years or so it has remained silent at times when it should have shouted. Its recent decision to downgrade the post of Director General gives cause for concern. Its President has argued both in the *Museums Journal*, and privately at York, that quiet diplomacy works, that confrontation with Government is self defeating. I don't believe this. The *Guardian* newspaper recently brought out a new Friday environmental section. It asked leading practitioners to tell readers what they were doing at present. Mrs Mary Whitehouse said that age and lack of energy had limited her gardening activities but that, in order to keep in touch morally and spiritually, she had taken to stroking tree trunks. I have to say that seductive though this practice might be, it doesn't get results. This is not the time, however aesthetic the thrill, for the Museum world to be stroking either tree-trunks or Ministers for the Arts.

It might appear churlish at this time to be criticising the Arts Minister who has been able to increase contributions both to the Arts Council, to National Museums and the Museums and Galleries Commission. I am sure that Nigel Pittman, the new Principal Finance Officer of the Office of Arts and Libraries, in his paper, does his best to convince us of the generosity of the gift and of the reality of the money. I remain unconvinced. I hope and understand that Scotland may have done better than England and Wales. If so I offer both my congratulations and my jealous curses. We should applaud the extra money granted to the building and maintenance programmes of national museums and galleries but I wonder if this covers the scale of the depredation wrought over generations by the Public Services Agency. I'm delighted to see the rise in grant to the MGC from £6.8 million this year to £10.2 million next year but I understand that some £3m of this money is earmarked to support the Horniman and Geffrye Museums. I am pleased for them but what is left? How much will trickle down to the Area Museum Councils and into the coffers of regional and local museums? If my grant is increased by 52% by the North of England Museums Service I could have at my disposal an extra £12,000 or so. Welcome but infinitesimal compared with the problems I've highlighted. It does seem as if the Government are not interested in the great majority of

local authority, regional and other museums. Unfortunately they ignore us at *our* peril. It all comes back to money, money, money.

In his introduction Trevor Clark waxes eloquent on the associations of music and money. Mozart and Beethoven competed with the strains of Sally Bowles. I was shocked, but not surprised, given the high seriousness of Scottish culture, that he missed the obvious musical cue. 'Strange' as Noel Coward said, 'the potency of cheap music'. Running through my mind is the tune of one of Abba's greatest hits, 'Money, Money, Money'. I quote wistfully that line that runs 'what a lot I could do if I had a little money in a rich man's world'. My academic background is literary rather than historical. I would like to indulge therefore in two small pieces of literary deconstruction. The first relates to an advertisement on the back of the winter edition of *Scottish Museum*

Museums Association Centenary Conference logo.

News. One of the Council's sponsors, The Scottish Mutual Assurance Society, pledges its support because, to quote, 'you've looked after our past'. I hope that reference in the past tense does not mean that they have lack of faith in your present or your future.

More seriously, I'd like to leave you with one last image. This is the logo that graced the Centenary Conference at York of the Museums Association. It is in the current free-flow-designer-brush-stroke style of corporate identities adopted by some museums. The Yorkshire Museum has just such a careless temple as its new image and recently the National History Museum, stamped its new name with a similarly styled logo. Its Director identified it as 'The Tree of Life' while its detractors called it the backside of a zebra. I don't seek to denigrate such institutions in their search for an identity which will attract new visitors but I do ask them to play devil's advocate on projected designs. Subconsciously such images can degrade the serious purpose of museums.

I would, therefore, like to provide a **reading** of the Museums Association's emblem. It combines tradition with trendiness. We have before us the archetypal museum, a temple set upon a hill — but its portico and roof are insecure, the supporting pillars, public and private finance perhaps, are askew. Unless museums are funded properly that door which appears to be half open will be seen to be slamming shut — and that **really** will be curatorial blood upon the steps.

The Main Hall of the Royal Museum of Scotland, Chambers Street, Edinburgh.

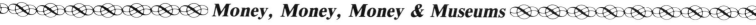

MUSEUMS AND CENTRAL GOVERNMENT FINANCIAL SUPPORT

Nigel Pittman was recently appointed Head of the Museums and Galleries Division and Principal Finance Officer of the Office of Arts and Libraries. At one time he was Private Secretary to Malcolm Rifkind MP. From 1980 he headed the branch of SED dealing with museums, galleries, libraries and the arts, and from 1985 was Museums Administrator and Secretary to the Trustees of the National Museums of Scotland.

This paper was written only a very short time after joining the Office of Arts and Libraries, so inevitably I may be a little imprecise in giving an overview of the Government's policies towards the funding of the museums and galleries sector and I will be restricting my remarks largely to the National Museums and Galleries scene. What I can do is to reflect a little on the experience of the last ten years and on my own perceptions of the changes which have taken place. They will be personal views and, insofar as this can ever be true of a civil servant, will not necessarily reflect unchanging Government policy. But I will also draw a little on the speech which the Minister for the Arts made to the Museums Association Conference in York, and of course refer to the settlement which he announced in November 1989 for the funding of the English Museums and Galleries.

First I want to mention two statements — or contentions — which were expressed at another important Conference in Edinburgh in November 1989. That was the Annual Conference of the Society of Antiquaries of Scotland. I want to commend the Society for its imagination and foresight in staging at this time a Conference on the theme 'A Future for the Past?' focusing on the growing tensions which exist within the so-called heritage industry between the more traditional museums and the new breed of 'heritage' theme parks.

It was a most stimulating, though sometimes infuriating, day, but during the course of it, I noted especially two comments made from the platform which, I suspect, no one in similar circumstances would have voiced ten years ago. One of the speakers, Dr Peter Addyman of the York Archaeological Trust, at one point referred to National Museums, like the British Museum and the National Museums of Scotland, as 'millstones round the necks of the taxpayers'. And in a slightly different context, Professor Peter Fowler said that it was well-known to be the Government's intention to phase out funding for museums and galleries within the next decade. What I want to do is to try to focus on the reasons why questions like these are being raised, and how the Government may be expected to respond to them.

My own direct experience of funding for Museums goes back only as far as 1980, but I thought it might be instructive to take a look at the sort of headlines and articles which were appearing in the press about museums in that year. So I got the Library at the Royal Museum to dig out its cuttings book for 1980 and I took a look through. Inevitably there is a strong bias towards the local interest issues — the exhibitions, lectures and so on which the Royal Museum was putting on that year — but there were also a few items reflecting on museums generally. What struck me was how little any flavour of controversy or change came across in those press reports. And that reflects my own memory of my first year or two in the Scottish Education Department (SED) dealing with the museums world. The battles were about very specific issues — would Glasgow University sell off its Whistlers; should the National Galleries of Scotland close some galleries at lunchtime in the winter months to save money — rather than about the overall drift of policies, financial or otherwise.

Looking through the headlines in the papers this year tells a very different story. Here is just a selection of headlines that I happened to lay my hands on:

Making a point about penury
'Neglected' V & A needs millions for repairs
Dark Deeds in the Great Bed of Ware
Massacre of the Scholars
Museums facing financial disaster
Museums beg Thatcher to ward off ruin
Castle Rackrent
Of Entrepreneurs and dinosaurs

What has made the press so interested in the state of museums? Of course, museums have become increasingly successful at using the press to draw attention to themselves, and stories about priceless treasures coming under threat, primarily because of the failings of generations of Ministers and civil servants to find adequate money to look after them, always make good copy. But this interest also reflects the underlying pace of change and the difficulties that it has brought in its wake. This decade has seen the most startling and far-reaching changes in the museums and galleries world, in every aspect of the way in which the institutions are run and the way in which they present themselves, probably since the middle of the nineteenth century. It is a

process of change for which many factors can be cited. Among them are the great growth of interest in museum and heritage-type attractions which arose from the leisure explosion of the 1970s, and the whole climate of greater awareness of management techniques and business skills which became the watchwords of the 1980s. But I would suggest that another key factor, whether arising from or leading these (and I think there has been a bit of both), is the way in which Government money has been used in this area over the last ten years.

Looking back now to 1980, it is hard to believe how straightforward was the process of deciding on the allocation of funds at that time. It wasn't very subtle. Usually it involved a standard uprating of the previous year's grant by an appropriate inflation factor, with a little tinkering here and there in recognition of some special case — usually the opening of a new gallery or building. Of course, there was never quite enough money. Both sides — the SED and the institutions (and here I include the Scottish Museums Council) — recognised that. But the debate about funding took the form of a kind of shadow-boxing. The institutions told SED what they thought they needed as extras. SED thought about it, then gave out what it could after the annual Public Expenditure round was complete. There was very little testing of assumptions, no questioning of objectives, little or no research into how effectively or otherwise money had been used in the past. One whole block of the money for the National Museums and Galleries — for the upkeep of the buildings — was simply handed over to another Government Department, the PSA, who proceeded to spend it as they thought fit. There were meetings to discuss progress on a broad programme of works. But I remember asking for a fully set-out programme of how the overall allocation was going to be used. There was consternation. No one ever asked that sort of question!

If this was the picture in the funding Department, what was it like on the other side of the fence? I can't speak for anywhere other than the constituent National Museums of Scotland, but there at least the handling of money and the understanding of how it should be used was rudimentary to say the least. That is hardly surprising when so little of the functional use was actually in the control of the institutions. Someone else looked after the buildings, ordered the furniture and some of the equipment, and most important paid for them. In the Royal Scottish Museum, which was still formally just a Division of the Scottish Office, someone else looked after the recruitment, pay and pensions of the staff — and again paid for it.

These two blocks of responsibility — buildings and staffing — made up, and still make up, the vast majority of the running costs. What was left was only the petty cash! And even that was treated rather haphazardly. At the National Museum of Antiquities for example the various sections of the museum weren't given specific budgets to work to; if there was an exhibition to be put on, they got on and arranged it. Someone else worried about the funding — or at least they did in theory. In practice the concern tended to be retrospective — and for several years the overspends had to be vired from purchase grants.

I don't want to give the impression that all museums went about things quite as haphazardly as that. But the point I want to make is that neither the civil servants in the funding Departments nor the staff of the museums tended to ask too many sophisticated questions about how the money was being used or whether the best possible value was being squeezed out of it. And there was of course also the almost unquestioned assumption that, because museums are manifestly for the public good, all the money would be Government money.

That is not to say that there were no exhibitions sponsored by other bodies. But in most instances when these did happen, it was a bit of a bonus and nothing to do with the continuum of life. And as for earning money, quite simply the system did everything it could

to discourage it. A notional target of 'receipts' was included in the Annual Supply Estimates. If you failed to reach it, your grant would stretch correspondingly less far. If you exceeded it, you had better spend the extra fast, because anything left at the end of the year would return to the Treasury. In England there was something called the 'revote', which meant that you might get any extra unspent receipts back in two years' time, but even then, though I do not think this was widely realised, these 'revotes' were not really additional funds at all, but were taken out of whatever total funds happened to be available.

It took some time before the Government's Financial Management Initiative began to filter down to the museums sector, but eventually it did. In a sense, everything which has happened over the last few years — and I am not suggesting that it has been entirely a smooth process — has stemmed from there. The emphasis has been first and foremost on establishing how the money which the Government provides is being used, and to ensure that it is directed in such a way that it makes the maximum possible impact. That is a process which is still very much evolving — and while things evolve, the process can often be a painful one. Changing a culture is never an easy matter, especially if that culture does not necessarily perceive that it needs to change and feels that inappropriate standards and techniques are being imposed upon it.

Let me run briefly through the various aspects of change. And here again I will be speaking specifically about the position in the National Museums and Galleries, which are directly funded from Government, though I am sure that those who work outwith that sector will recognise many of the signs.

The overall direction has been to give each institution a real sense of responsibility for *all* of the assets at its command. Traditionally, that responsibility was exercised primarily over the collections. Of course, the collections remain the central issue — though I am aware that many people have questioned whether that is still so. Without them, none of the infrastructure of staff, buildings and equipment would be necessary. But because they are necessary, someone has to manage them. It has been the Government's view that the only sensible place for them to be managed is from within the institutions themselves. That requires that all the facts are available to the managers and all the responsibilities rest with them. A complication about many of the problems which the press has highlighted in the last few years has been that too many things were not precisely known: what it really cost to preserve the collections, to maintain the buildings, to pay the staff. Much of the direction of Government policy, at least since 1983, has been to put Museums in a position where they could really assess the size of the task they faced in managing what they had got, and developing and presenting it in a way which benefits all the publics which potentially they serve.

I mention 1983 because that was the year when the two big Departmental Museums in England — the V & A and the Science Museum — became Trustee-led bodies. That change, although it directly affected only two institutions — the similar move for the Royal Scottish Museum came two years later, coupled of course with an amalgamation — had far-reaching consequences for the whole sector. Gradually the nature of the Boards of Trustees of the other institutions has also changed.

Trustees have been encouraged generally to take a more active, interventionist part at the strategic level in the direction of the institutions they are appointed to. They are expected now to debate actively the objectives for the institution and to review its direction at regular intervals. This of course can be difficult, both for Trustees themselves and for the institution's management, but Trustees can be an enormous strength. That happens where they have particular expertise, or can facilitate contacts, which the institution itself could not otherwise call on.

Much too depends on the amount of time they can give to understanding the institution's particular needs. We were extremely fortunate at the National Museums of Scotland in that the core of the initial Board of Trustees consisted of eight people who had spent a very thorough year learning about the work of the Museums as members of Lord Bute's Museums Advisory Board. Their knowledge was invaluable in providing a sense of direction for the National Museums of Scotland, and the institution was seriously weakened when four of them had to stand down after the first two years. What must be understood is that it takes time to assess the nature and essential needs of an institution like this, and, once gained, that knowledge should not be lightly cast aside.

The major documents to which Boards of Trustees are now asked to put their names on behalf of the National Museums and Galleries are the Corporate, or Financial, Plans. And I know that increasingly these are being introduced as important management tools throughout the Museums sector. From Government's point of view, the Plans are now seen as the key documents in the process of considering funding requirements for the Museums and Galleries. They have replaced the earlier system of Estimate bids and have become the formal channel for the expression of the Museum's aspirations and objectives. They also set the goals and targets against which the success or otherwise of the institution will to a large degree be measured.

The production of the Annual Financial Plan has now become the chief focus of management activity within many institutions. It uses up a considerable amount of staff time, and many people remain rather sceptical about the value of the exercise. It seems to me that there are two things which must be seen to happen if there isn't to be a gradual falling-off again in commitment to the production of such Plans. One, quite obviously, is that a genuine dialogue should take place on the basis of the Plans, and that when Government cannot respond to a fully-argued case for help, the reasons why are explained and discussed.

Museum of Flight, East Fortune, general view of hangar.

The other thing which must occur if the Plans are to go on gaining in value is that they must be used **within** the organisation which produces them. They must be an expression of the organisation's aspirations and intentions to which all staff pay a good deal more than lip-service. The Government indicates certain points on which it would like the institutions to focus attention, but it prefers now to let the actual format of the plans be a matter for the institution itself to decide in its own circumstances. Nothing is more likely to engender cynicism and apathy than the knowledge that Plans are being produced just for the Government's consumption and that the organisation is nevertheless proceeding to act in a totally different way from what the Plan says it will. So, for the investment of time and thought to be worthwhile, all staff must be made to feel that they have a part to play in the process of producing the Plans and that they are equally a part of what goes on after the Plan is submitted. Their objectives must in other words fit within the framework the Plan creates and their use

of resources must take account of the organisation's needs as a whole, as expressed in the Plan.

Among the requirements which go along with the production of Plans are those favourite management tools: performance measurement; and the setting of priorities and objectives. I would not suggest that institutions did not in the past ask themselves the questions: What are we here to do? What do we want to achieve over the next five or ten years? But there was perhaps more of an implicit assumption that everyone knew the answers anyway, so what was the point of setting them down. The process of asking the questions has, I suspect, surprised some organisations into a recognition that they didn't actually have a particularly clear answer, or that the answer today was not the one they had decided on some years ago. You may wonder what that has got to do with Government money, but the fact must be faced that you would not purchase a product in the shops without knowing just what you were buying. Why should the Government, on behalf of the taxpayer — or indeed any other potential investor in Museums — sink money endlessly into a concern unless it was sure it knew what that concern thought it could deliver?

And it is not of course just a matter of what the institutions think they could deliver, but whether they are going to be capable of doing so and, after the event, whether they have in fact done so. How to measure these things in the case of Museums is a question which has provoked endless debate over the last few years. The inclusion of a need for 'performance measures' in the Government's requests for Financial Plans has caused a certain amount of controversy and even suspicion. The controversy is not so much about the need for measures per se, but about which measures are sought — and how they should be used.

It has to be recognised that measures can be useful in different ways for different recipients, and that what a Museum or Gallery may find of most internal use may not be a particularly valuable indicator for its funding body. I myself have no doubt that, if used intelligently and sensitively, performance measures can be good indicators of health and performance for both sides. But, crucially, the measures need to be taken together with other factors — for example, to put it in its crudest terms, an indicator of the number of visitors through the door will mean little if the factors affecting those numbers (like the possible closure of large areas of the building for roofworks) are not also taken into account. And most measures need to be taken over a period of years, especially if they are to be used to judge success in achieving stated long-term objectives. In other words, they require patience and flexibility on behalf of the body which does the monitoring.

If this patience and flexibility is to be forthcoming, there has to be from the recipient's side a commitment that the continuing supply of finance is going to be well managed. All contributors, whether in Government or the private sector, have a right to expect that the resources they put up will be prudently and thoughtfully deployed, and that they can be fully and adequately accounted for. Hence the concentration of concern over the last few years on improved financial management within institutions.

There are those, I know, who think that has gone too far. They talk of large armies of bureaucrats 'providing all possible assistance short of actual help' taking over the running of museums, and of money which would have been available to spend on purchases or research being channelled instead into paying the inflated salaries of accountants and administrators. Well, you wouldn't expect me to accept that point of view, would you? But on the other hand I appreciate the fears it expresses and the underlying concern that exists about a shift of balance within Museums.

In response I must point out that the level of financial acumen in most Museums was until recently derisory. There were honourable exceptions. But very few

A young participant in Kirkpatrick MacMillan rally in 1990.

institutions had in place systems of control and monitoring which were entirely appropriate for the large quantities of taxpayers and private money passing through their hands. All of that is now changing, but setting up and operating adequate systems inevitably requires some increase in staff to run them. Provided the staff are well chosen and the selection of systems is carefully handled, I have no doubt that the diversion of resources will prove to be an investment which in a few years time will be so much a part of the fabric that no one will believe it could ever have raised eyebrows.

I have spoken so far about a range of general points which the Government has been keen to see incorporated in the way in which Museums and Galleries are organised, with the aim of assuring itself, and the taxpayer, that resources are used for agreed and understood objectives, and to the maximum benefit. But the Government also uses part of its money to concentrate on very specific issues where it believes that there is a need, either in the short or the longer term, for particular help. Increasingly in the last few years it has used its money in this way as seed-corn to get developments under way, with the prospect either that the development will produce long-term savings throughout the Museum, or that others will be encouraged to come on board with help which they might not otherwise have given.

In the first category I would put the investment here by SED in the National Museums' proposals for a computerised documentation system for the collections. This was proposed by the Trustees from the first as a major priority. In 1987-88, SED and NMS jointly put in £200,000 to enable the project to get off the ground, and since then progress has been so rapid that the National Museums are looking at the completion of the primary database by 1994, and at the possibility of offering a major public Information Centre facility based on it in the new Museum of Scotland. At the same time, NMS is already providing a service to the National Galleries of Scotland, and is in the process of offering facilities to other museums and similar bodies throughout Scotland.

In the second category, Government has put forward money in recent years for a variety of schemes, such as the Business Sponsorship Incentive Scheme and the Museum Marketing Consultancy Scheme, which are aimed at giving museums and galleries the chance to benefit from tapping into other sources of funding, or of improving their ability to generate receipts. At the same time it has channelled funds through the Museums and Galleries Commission, for instance to help set up the Conservation Unit in 1987 and, more recently, the Travelling Exhibitions Unit.

The latest example of this special targeting of funds is the commitment which has been made, together with the Museums Association, to establish the Museum Training Institute. I have no doubt that the business of training museum staff to meet the needs of the fast-moving world in which they increasingly find themselves is one which most of us have tended to overlook, or to pay at best token attention to, as the President of the Museums Association pointedly made clear in his address to the Association's Conference in September 1989. The Government, through the OAL, paid for the production earlier in 1989 of the MTI's first business plan and also committed in 1989-90 £150,000 to the establishment of the Institute, with promises of further funding for the forward years. The Training Agency also contributed about £50,000 in 1989-90 to various MTI costs including training the MTI staff and preparing publicity material/information packs. The range of activities in which Simon Roodhouse, the MTI's Director, is aiming to become involved is impressive and I hope that, for the sake of the future health of the museums profession, the Institute will become a success and will get the support of all.

The establishment of the Institute was just one of the developments to which the Minister for the Arts referred most warmly in his keynote address to the Museums Association Conference in York. And I want now just to recap on some of the things he said. The theme of the Conference of course was 'Museums Open for Business', which is perhaps just another way of saying 'Money, Money, Money and Museums', and he referred to the increasing moves towards greater self-reliance and plural funding which museums and galleries have adopted in both the public and the private sectors. But he went on to say:

'But increased freedom does not mean less support. While we look to the museums to develop greater self-reliance the Government believes that support from the taxpayer is also fundamental to their wellbeing. In our 1987 Election Manifesto, we pledged ourselves to maintain Government support for the arts and we have repeatedly reaffirmed that commitment. That is our side of the bargain.'

The Minister followed up that statement by positive action in the form of the revised three-year funding settlement which he announced on 16th November 1989. There had been repeated cries over the past year that the basis for the three-year funding which he introduced in 1987-88 was being significantly eroded by the increase in inflation. The Minister was able to show that, when such erosion was recognised to be taking place, the Government was in a position to respond and to restore the position. Indeed he did more than that. Since I have quoted some of the adverse headlines, let me now quote one or two positive ones from papers commenting on the announcement:

Recognition of the Artistic Imperative
Backing Success
The Begging Bowls are Brimming

This settlement is a very important sign, not just for the present round of funding, but also for the future. It should give the Museums and Galleries, and indeed the arts world in general, the assurance that, where necessary, levels of funding can and will be looked at again, even within the framework of a three-year settlement, when unforeseen factors come into play.

A good deal of the extra funding the Minister announced was in the buildings grants for the National Museums and Galleries. This too was an area of concern which he foreshadowed in his York speech. There he spoke of his ambition 'to see the basic fabric of our National Museums and Galleries in tip-top condition by the end of the century'. And he urged that all possible sources of funding — patronage, bequests, sponsorship and endowment funding — should be tapped to enable this objective to be achieved.

The handing-over of responsibility for the buildings they occupy to the institutions themselves and to their Boards of Trustees, achieved over the last two years, has meant that each of them is now assessing for themselves the maintenance and building needs which face them. In some cases — the Royal Museum of Scotland and other buildings which the National Museums of Scotland occupy, are a case in point — the prospect is an extremely daunting one. But it is only by first thoroughly identifying the problem and then setting about systematically tackling it, that real prospects of success can be envisaged. The Government's commitment — evidenced by a 19% increase for next year in the sums to be allocated to NMG Building Programmes — is fundamental here, and there are beginning to be signs that it is attracting other support, even for the less glamorous sorts of work. The property firm, MEPC plc, has given £1m over five years (to be matched by Government money) for repairs to the Sir John Soane's Museum in London; and the Wolfson Trusts have donated £2m a year for three years (again matched by Government money) for refurbishment of displays within museums and galleries.

Finally, in his speech the Minister reflected on the nature of the challenge for museums and galleries to which ultimately all policies are directed. This is how he defined it:

'I believe that our chief concerns must be the **spread of excellence** and the strengthening of scholarship and research. All management changes, all marketing schemes, all training initiatives must be dedicated to these objectives. They must fulfil the twin aims of supporting and enhancing scholarship while making its fruits more available to the public.

Museums are a gateway to education, information and enjoyment, a gateway that must be open to all.

Gavin Sprott, curator at the Scottish Agricultural Museum, Ingliston, with a young visitor.

Our aim must be to make the best of our arts, the treasures of our museums and all the riches of scholarship available to more and more people.

These things are not a private preserve, open only to the scholastic elite, from which the rest of us are barred. Of course we need the elite to demand and practise the highest standards of excellence. But we need them too to help break down the barriers, to make the collections they treasure meaningful to the rest of us.'

And he went on to say:

'If the museums failed to rise to this challenge by turning in on themselves and refusing to share their cultural richness; if they were so limited as to say or imply by their actions that scholarship is only for scholars; then they would rapidly lose public esteem. They would find little support coming to them directly from the public. And they would themselves be calling into question that support which they receive from the taxpayer.'

That then is the nature of the challenge as the Minister sees it. He has, I think, made it quite clear what for him is the agenda for the next few years. He has reiterated a pledge to continuing levels of Government support for the Museums and Galleries and suggested what he believes that support is ultimately aimed at achieving. The recent financial settlement shows that he is able to deliver the additional help which is needed when difficulties arise, though I know that there are still those who will argue that there should be more — for instance, on purchase grants, as we have heard. But even for them there was perhaps a note of hope in the Minister's speech when he said that 'the arts is no longer the Cinderella of the political world'. And I notice that that is something taken up by Peter Palumbo in an article in *The Times* when he pledged himself 'to get the arts firmly and irrevocably on the political agenda of our times'.

Whatever the implications of that, there is no doubt in my mind that the changes which have taken place in the museums world over the last ten, and especially the last five years, will prove in the long term to be beneficial ones. For all the heartaches that have sometimes been caused, and still are being caused, the opening-up to a greater variety of funding sources, the increased awareness of the need for agreed objectives and more prudent and thoughtful management of resources, are the firm basis on which the continuing excellence of the museums sector is being built. Museums and galleries have so much to offer to so many people that, whatever the problems they encounter along the way, their fundamental appeal to our requirement for knowledge, enjoyment and a sense of the richness and variety of life both in the past and in the future must continue to argue their case for a share of the 'wealth of a nation'.

I want to end with a short poem by W B Yeats, partly because it is so much more eloquent than anything I can myself write; partly because, despite the decidedly patrician attitude it adopts, I think it contains a message which is as relevant to Governments or to private donors and sponsors who plan to invest in museums and galleries. It has one of the longest titles of any poem I know but at least it makes its own agenda very clear from the start.

To a wealthy man who promised a second subscription to the Dublin Municipal Gallery if it were proved the people wanted pictures

YOU gave, but will not give again
Until enough of Paudeen's pence
By Biddy's halfpennies have lain
To be 'some sort of evidence',
Before you'll put your guineas down,
That things it were a pride to give
Are what the blind and ignorant town
Imagines best to make it thrive.

What cared Duke Ercole, that bid
His mummers to the market-place,
What th' onion-sellers thought or did
So that his Plautus set the pace
For the Italian comedies?

And Guidobaldo, when he made
That grammar school of courtesies
Where wit and beauty learned their trade
Upon Urbino's windy hill,
Had sent no runners to and fro
That he might learn the Shepherds' will,
And when they drove out Cosimo,
Indifferent how the rancour ran,
He gave the hours they had set free
To Michelozzo's latest plan
For the San Marco Library,

Whence turbulent Italy should draw
Delight in Art whose end is peace,
In logic and in natural law
By sucking at the dugs of Greece.

Your open hand but shows our loss,
For he knew better how to live.
Let Paudeens play at pitch and toss,
Look up in the sun's eye and give
What the exultant heart calls good
That some new day may breed the best
Because you gave, not what they would,
But the right twigs for an eagle's nest!

'The Right Twigs for an Eagle's Nest' isn't a bad way to
think about 'Money and Museums'!

Dundee Waterfront Development showing Discovery Quay from the east.

PARTNERSHIP FUNDING IN THE PRIVATE AND PUBLIC SECTORS

Jonathan Bryant, Chief Executive, Dundee Industrial Heritage Ltd, is responsible for Scott's research ship *Discovery* and is developing museum and heritage attractions for Dundee. He is Secretary of the Association of Independent Museums.

It is encouraging that this publication is looking not only at how to increase resources for museums but how to use these more effectively and responsibly. I noted with interest the terms which Nigel Pittman used to describe museums' understanding of money. They ranged from rudimentary to derisory!

The title of this section is perplexing. Let us start with two definitions. The Private Sector I regard as the area of non-charitable, non-voluntary activity. It includes business, commerce and industry, which collectively keep our economy afloat. In the Public Sector falls expenditure by central or local government and those non-elected bodies which are funded by either or both sources.

I have always worked within independent museums of which there are a number of distinct types. One of these was truly in the private sector, a museum of beer wholly owned by one of the big six brewers. This was under the direct control of its parent and founding company whose objectives it was ultimately there to meet. Subsequently I have been involved exclusively in the charitable independent museum. Each has had its own memorandum and articles of association and a board of directors and trustees representing a range of interests

including the private, the public and the voluntary sectors.

I am not able to share with you experience of partnership funding in the private sector. I have none and I know of few cases which are relevant for discussion. Neither am I able to speak about partnership funding for museums in the public sector. Peter Lewis of Beamish is in a much better position to do so. What I can do is speak up for the middle ground and outline both the potential and the dilemmas of simultaneous public and private sector feet. What I want to do is explore the benefits and frustrations of curatorial polygamy.

I do not intend to discuss commercial sponsorship, charitable giving and other such mechanisms for private sector involvement, participation in and contribution to museum activities. This receives a pretty good airing wherever you go these days and we are all in our own ways getting better at it, even if more slowly than some would wish. Neither do I intend to cover some of the excellent partnership arrangements which exist between local authorities and groupings of the smaller independent museums in particular. In such cases, the sharing of human resources and expertise rather than cash often provide interesting formulae for success and especially in Scotland.

What I am going to talk about is development. Like 'community' and 'environment', 'development' is a fine word. It provides some comfort while carefully concealing its full intention.

What sort of development? I have in mind the Royal Opera House plan to finance its refurbishment through permissions for general shopping and office use in its rebuilt and extended spaces. The Royal Opera House has to reconcile its own technical requirements with the cost of meeting these when it has land but no cash. There are many property developments which offer benefits to socially desirable or not-for-profit groups who grasp such opportunities to improve their own position. These arrangements appear attractive to the private sector developer since they bring both people and general acceptability to shops, offices, bars and the consequent architectural monuments to mammon. Their ultimate purpose is to secure planning permission.

A current planning application for a drive-in McDonalds on the outskirts of Dundee is associated with 'recreational use'. This is perceived favourably by local authorities because until recently they could afford to and were themselves expected to provide most recreational facilities.

What has this got to do with museums? Developments and planning applications like this have a lot to do with maritime museums in Barrow-in-Furness and Anstruther; a lot to do with emigration centres in Greenock and historic dockyards at both Portsmouth and Chatham. They have more than a lot to do with Captain Scott's Antarctic Exploration Ship *Discovery*, built in Dundee in 1901 and I will use, by way of illustration, examples from my own experience.

I wonder whether commercial property developments, may offer solutions to the numerous structural problems faced by our major institutions. In the national museums leaking roofs are fashionable just now. British Rail finance the upgrading of their mainline terminals by building offices and hotels over the top and that certainly keeps the passengers dry! Walking along Chambers Street recently I noted that Robert Anderson had the East Wing of the Royal Museum heavily scaffolded. Surely the public have a right to know!

However, we should not be too bullish, the property development world is not what it was, even six months ago. Higher interest rates, sluggish retail sales, a fear of overcapacity and I suspect, a speciality shopping, fast food and multiscreen cinema formula whose popularity has peaked, do not encourage optimism at the present time. By definition the private sector property market has a much speedier response to cyclic economic changes than museums. Keeping pace with mammon can be a problem.

Partnership funding in the private and public sectors, the subject of this section deserves, I feel, a better working title. The Art Of The Deal will do nicely. A summary of our own position in Dundee will prove helpful as we work through some of the issues involved.

Firstly some background to our organisation. The parent body is The Dundee Heritage Trust which was formed in 1985 from a community committee that had collected examples of jute and linen working machinery. Represented on the Board of Trustees are the City of Dundee District Council, Tayside Regional Council, the University of Dundee, Trades Unions, Chamber of Commerce and importantly, the private sector in the form of leading figures from local industry and commerce.

The Trust establishes policy and raises funds only. It does not execute that policy or 'trade' in any sense. Rather, it operates through a wholly owned subsidiary company, Dundee Industrial Heritage Ltd. This excellent arrangement not only limits the liability of those

Discovery's stern before clearing marine growth in 1986.

through sponsorships, admissions and sales. The remaining income is in the form of temporary public sector subsidy.

There are three principal areas of activity.

Firstly, we will establish a museum of Dundee's jute and linen industry based on both the existing collection and the acquisition of an appropriate site and buildings.

Secondly, we are the custodians of Royal Research Ship *Discovery*. A full restoration programme has commenced and at the same time the historic vessel is being developed as a visitor and community resource.

Thirdly, the Trust is working with both the public and private sectors to secure an advantageous new berth for *Discovery* and provide associated public and visitor facilities. It is this third project and the way in which it has been approached that we will examine in some detail.

In 1979 *Discovery* was saved from destruction by the Maritime Trust which subsequently assembled a collection of historic ships in St Katherine's Dock, by the Tower Bridge in London. The St Katherine's Dock property development has been very successful for its developer and includes the World Trade Centre. Its tenant cafes, bars, souvenir shops, restaurants, offices and conference facilities have benefited enormously from the presence of historic ships. Unfortunately the ships fared less well. The development levied a hefty berthing fee without providing parking, signing, toilets or other essential services. Attracted by the 'heritage component' thousands of tourists annually enjoyed the ships from a distance. They did not pay admission fees to visit and support the vessels.

Since the early 1980s, the authorities in Dundee had been planning a future for a large area of waterfront between the City's River Tay rail and road bridges. Although unused for many years, the 30-acre site is

Trustees who are also Company Directors but also provides protection for the Trust itself. Significantly the Trust's second subsidiary company owns the collections and does not trade. The 'heritage' assets therefore, are given every possible protection in law.

The Trust raises funds through a separate Development Committee and has a membership scheme comprising Friends (volunteers) and Supporters (revenue generation). To put some financial dimension to this picture we have an overall turnover of about £450,000 per annum. One third of this is raised charitably and one third is earned magnificently situated offering exceptional potential if imaginations might be sparked and private investment encouraged. *Discovery* was identified as an enabling ingredient, legal and financial agreements reached with the Maritime Trust and Dundee Heritage Trust took the project on.

Discovery returned home during April 1986 and Dundee Industrial Heritage Ltd assumed immediate responsibility for her. The move was not without its practical, financial and political problems. These were overcome with substantial help from the Scottish Development Agency and the City of Dundee District Council. Dundee Port Authority kindly offered free temporary berthing in Victoria Dock.

We have commenced a lengthy restoration programme involving, substantial areas of the ship's structure, all internal fixtures and fittings and the essential plant and services required to prepare her for long-term public appreciation and use. We also offer an annual visitor season and have established shore-based reception, exhibition and sales areas of a temporary though reasonable standard. Guided tours of the vessel are complemented by specific projects at peak times. The introduction of theatre, for example, has helped to bring alive interiors which otherwise appear at best unconvincing and at worst sterile. These programmes have been possible only with private sector sponsorship and Regional Council support of their educational benefits.

Partnership With Whom For What?

There are many different interests represented in the partnership arena. A partner can be a;

Person associated with others in business sharing both risks and profits. How many museums are prepared to expose principles to risk in order to reap benefits for them?

Wife or husband. We all know that these partnerships are never as smooth as we might wish.

Companion in a game or dance. Property developments are certainly games of chance and at times a merry dance as well. If you have not played before you are at a distinct disadvantage. Having two left feet does not help!

Timber framework round hole in deck. This definition came as news to me but it is not inappropriate in our case.

Mutual Objectives or Agreed Compromise?

Who are the various parties that come together seeking to achieve their individual sets of objectives through partnership? Are the objectives compatible or do they inevitably require some form of compromise?

Central Government's policy is clearly to reduce public commitments, to encourage private participation and to promote self-help and enterprise. **Development Corporations or Agencies** exist to rectify problems of market failure and to act as a private sector catalyst. Characteristically, development agencies move quickly. Too quickly sometimes to take full account of local sensitivities and often they seek copy cat solutions to economic and development problems. There are various categories of commerical **Property Developer.** The thoroughbred deserves every million he earns through personal risk and corporate exposure. At the other end of the spectrum are those who use only other people's money and do not put bricks in place until their positions are totally secured. **Regional or County** authorities are key players in the development game. They are responsible for infrastructure, roads, water supplies and sewers. Without vital services nothing can be done. The role of the **Institutions** which ultimately provide the private sector capital, is to maximise the return for pension fund investors, building society deposit holders and other investors. **District Councils**

Launch of special Keiller's marmalade pots at sales point.

are responsible for local planning issues. In Scotland they are also responsible for leisure, recreation, museums and tourism. **Politicians** are a fact of life and always with us. If a partnership does not work they will have told us so. When it is successful they cut the ribbon and let the world know what has been achieved. Election time is testing time for public/private sector partnerships of all descriptions. **Careers** are to be made in partnership projects and especially where heritage is concerned. Like shopping and eating out, everyone has a strong opinion about it. **Consumers** are the final users. In the community context, property developments rarely represent the highest aspirations of local communities and conservation issues inevitably rear their head. Lastly there are **Ourselves**, the museum or heritage groups seeking to find expression for our ideals.

What The Market Left Undone

An aerial view of Dundee's waterfront shows a magnificent site but one that has been a problem for most of this century. Enterprising proposals for it, The Central Waterfront Improvement Scheme, were put forward in 1912 by the then City Engineer, James Thomson. His vision of the future included expansive parkland and promenade areas; the first road bridge across the Tay, a single carriageway built on the stumps of the original and collapsed Rail Bridge; a new terminal station at Dundee West; splendid accommodation for the Dundee Port Authority and dignified civic premises in place of the present City Square and Caird Hall.

But none of this came about. The scheme was beyond the civic purse. Dundee's business community could not justify private development and there were no carrots tempting enough to attract outside investment at that time. Instead the area which includes dockland, railway sidings, ferry terminal and esplanade eventually became waste. Earlier development of Dundee's waterfront was prevented by the problems of multi-ownership; contamination levels; servicing costs; general economic and image problems.

Before any successful development project can proceed a climate which encourages partnership has to be created. The principle is to turn problems into opportunities, pool resources and make things happen.

Creating The Climate

The first step is to turn problems into opportunities and make them both practically and financially attractive to the private sector. This is done by the assembly of land into one, development friendly, ownership and by its enterprise zone designation. Enterprise zones are now less favoured by central government but incentives include reduced planning controls, tax incentives and rate free holidays. Needless to say the selection of enterprise zones

Her Majesty the Queen meets volunteers and crew aboard *Discovery* on 1st July 1987.

and their boundaries have been a source of much debate and frustration.

Good marketing is being different. An excellent climate creator is the identification of a 'story to be told'. A unique story can set one project apart from others. It can also bring different interests together on neutral ground and with a sense of common purpose. A good interpretive theme encourages the visualisation of a desirable finished product. At its extreme, story boarding can transform the severest problem into a heritage concept. So remember, don't let facts get in the way of a good theme!

A range of illustrations prepared by Don Aldridge shows not only the importance of ships and the sea to Dundee but how *Discovery*, built in the City in 1901, is a powerful national symbol around which much of the community's industrial heritage can be presented.

Levering Out The Development Dollar

The job of attracting private investment begins as land is assembled and development briefs prepared. Value can be unlocked in many ways. Local planning guidelines may be reviewed; perceptions of dereliction can be changed and in exchange for jobs created the public sector may invest heavily in both set up and infrastructure costs.

A topical example of the unlocking principle is selling off water services in England and Wales. The water authorities have vast areas of highly desirable land whose commercial potential is not exploited because management has been too busy supplying water. Soon however, development opportunities and heritage sites of all descriptions will spring up around reservoirs in England and Wales. Similar 'value' is currently extracted from hospital foyers where franchises are let for shopping of all types.

Responding to the brief, interested developers offer a variety of uses and attempt to maximise the perceived desirability of their plans by offering incentives of community benefit. In our own case the requirement was precise. The development brief specified a visitor centre adjacent to Royal Research Ship *Discovery* and an annual cash sum to help support the maintenance costs of the historic ship. Both were offered.

The total cost of Discovery Quay is in excess of £45m. Of this the public sector are contributing between £6m and £7m. This gearing, the relationship between public and private funds employed, is 1 to 6, a ratio well in line with government expectations. However there may be many hidden public sector costs, including salaries, professional fees and other expenses.

Planning Gain

Planning gain is the principle which drives these developments forward. The development is granted planning permission for things not otherwise possible in exchange for buildings, services or cash benefits which are seen to be socially desirable. Often the permission is for retail units. In Dundee's case for a 65,000 sq ft food store and a smaller DIY retail warehouse, both enjoying excellent location and access.

Discovery's new dock has been built by the Scottish Development Agency. It is part of the public sector investment. The developer has undertaken to provide the built shell of our Discovery Quay Visitor Centre (23,000 sq ft) at an assumed cost of £3m and to contribute £50,000 per annum for 15 years towards the maintenance and upkeep of the ship. You will immediately recognise the difference between this arrangement and that which *Discovery* previously endured in St Katherine's Dock, London.

Effectively the Discovery Quay developer is paying for both retail permissions and the appeal that Royal Research Ship *Discovery* brings to the cafes, bars, speciality shops, night club and cinema which are leased to others. Clearly *Discovery* can benefit substantially from the greater flows of people who will use the total provision. Both feed each other and the benefits are mutual.

No Such Thing As A Free Museum

The developer does not pay for the fitting out of the Discovery Quay museum or visitor centre. These are additional costs which must be met. A substantial cost to the public sector sponsors and to an independent trust working within the partnership, is lack of control over the specification, design and build processes.

Who Pays The Piper? Who Calls The Tune?

Control mechanisms can be complicated. Unless considerable care is taken they become less than satisfactory. The developer will have his own architects and professional team; the public sector their own civil engineers and quantity surveyors. The attractiveness of the 'heritage component' is both strength and weakness simultaneously. Every partner seeks to influence its concept, design and execution.

Learning The Jargon. Policing the Action

Most enterprising activities breed their own jargon and property development is no exception. At one time we

Sir Peter Scott in front of *Discovery* at the launch of the Dundee Heritage Club, 21st April 1987.

the private sector delivers what it has undertaken to provide.

A condition of the private/public sector agreement for Dundee's Discovery Quay was that no start should be made to the food store for Tesco until a start had been made on *Discovery's* visitor centre. Technically this has been complied with. However Tesco will be trading by Easter 1990 and the visitor centre has yet to take physical form. It has been further agreed that the visitor facility should be operable within a specified period of time.

I know of some instances in which Developers have reneged completely on their commitments. I am pleased to say that in Dundee the development premium has been secured in cash, and is invested awaiting a start to build date. It is currently estimated that the Discovery Quay centre can be completed by early 1992.

Keeping Pace With Change

Raising interest rates, changes in the leisure industry and reduced speciality retail sales have in part been responsible for delays in progressing our own interests in Discovery Quay. Design alterations have also created difficulties for the local authorities. No less important however, have been changes in the market for multiscreen cinemas and fast foods courts whose operators constantly review investment decisions. New tenants are now sought to replace those end users originally committed to the cinema, restaurant and night club at Discovery Quay.

What will happen to socially desirable features once a commercial development has exhausted its business and fashion cycle? This question is not resolved. The best developments may have retained some worthwhile fabric of the built environment which would not otherwise have been possible. In other cases a finite lifetime may be preferable.

went to the shop for a pint of milk or a loaf of bread. Now it is the retail element! The serious point is that it is not sufficient to rehearse the nomenclature for meetings and presentations. Dealing with commercial property developers is a tough business. We must acquire skills to police these situations effectively and ensure that

Short Term Products Or Lasting Assets?

Discovery Quay Development is entirely new build. It does not conserve or retain buildings of any type. It is estimated that its commercial lifetime will be 12 years after which substantial changes will be required. Nevertheless its planning and development have greatly assisted our own organisation and helped us to achieve a platform for and commitment to the City's industrial past that would not otherwise have been possible.

Dundee Heritage Trust is currently considering the acquisition of a compact and historically intact jute and linen works which requires substantial restoration. This could become the museum of Dundee's textile industry. The concept for this is a broad one, far exceeding original aspirations for the modest collection with which we started. Such confidence would not have been possible without the return of *Discovery* and the Discovery Quay Development which secured this financially. Dundee's new status as City of Discovery has and continues to inspire a wide range of cultural initiatives. Witches Blood proved a community drama of epic proportion and firework spectaculars are an annual event.

Whose Balance Sheet?

We have discussed the unlocking of value and the releasing of assets. Finally we might consider on whose balance sheet which assets should appear.

The developer of Discovery Quay, Tesco, and other tenants will pay for the presence of Royal Research Ship *Discovery* and theming of the development. Scott's Antarctic exploration vessel and its story are an asset to them. I doubt whether a notional value of *Discovery's* appeal is included in Tesco's balance sheet but it is an interesting point and we are taking it up with them. Perhaps too, we should consider placing a value for Tesco in the balance sheet of our own trading Company. It is not a cultural or heritage asset but it will

Staff, assisting at the launch of the Goodfellow and Steven *Discovery* range, on board *RRS Discovery*, 1988.

bring many hundreds of thousands of people a year to Discovery Quay and this is clearly important to us.

If such thoughts appear fanciful here is one last illustration announcing what Tottenham Hotspur now does with the valuable players it transfers from other clubs. It even depreciates them as their legs slow down and the grey hairs appear!

Conclusion

We have examined the potential partnerships for museums in property developments involving both the private and public sectors and have considered the substantial benefits which can accrue. In practice however, the issues are not as easily controllable as we would wish. There are in this respect many lessons yet to be learned.

I believe that the custodians of our cultural heritage will have to arm themselves with many more methods of financing future projects. Good housekeeping alone will not support our interests against the ever increasing demands on traditional sources of funding for museums and the arts.

A MUSIC at OXFORD concert in the Sheldonian Theatre, Oxford.

Stephen Mayes.

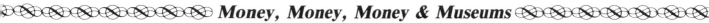

DEVELOPING RESOURCES FOR THE ARTS FROM SCRATCH

Hanya Chlala.

Karen Gadd, Managing Director, MUSIC
at OXFORD, organised her first series of concerts
in Oxford in 1983. MUSIC at OXFORD
presented 108 concerts in 1989, financed by ticket
sales and sponsorship. Karen Gadd believes that
government subsidy of the arts is essential.

I have been involved in raising sponsorship since 1983. I believe in sponsorship as means of raising considerable sums for the Arts but more importantly I believe in it as a corporate activity. In Britain we seem to regard the creation of wealth as an almost indecent activity, which is at its most extreme in our scorn of self-made millionaires. It is regarded as more respectable to enter any profession, even the arts, than become a professional engineer. Very strange, even stranger is the horror of anything labelled commercial. **Music at Oxford**, a charity promoting over 120 concerts a year, is regarded as commercial because our marketing is high profile and effective, and because we receive our funding from sponsors and audiences. In the mysterious world of arts funding to be labelled commercial is the kiss of death, hence we remain unfunded.

In many ways for **Music at Oxford** it is better for us to put our future in the hands of sponsors than government, because with a very small amount of financial acumen one can understand the rules. In my experience sponsors are fair, honourable, helpful, and supportive. But as in any sensitive relationship it is important to understand and try and fulfil each other's expectations.

The only frustration I feel about sponsorship is that

there is so much out there and I don't move fast enough to gather all I need in. It is not easy to raise, but it is certainly available.

This is its main advantage over funding. Sponsorship is not a finite source of income. It is there in its billions to be found, cultivated, grown and created. This is the positive aspect of corporate funding. Corporate sponsorship has a large role to play in funding certain segments of the arts and museum activities. But it is not a balanced form of funding, it certainly does not replace public funding. Whereas government funding is a very finite and diminishing source of income to the arts, sponsorship grows and expands. To encourage this sponsorship to become more accessible, certain actions are needed. These include:

a. Serious and simple tax incentives to encourage a much higher level of corporate sponsorship and donations.

b. Arts organisations need to organise themselves both collectively and individually to encourage local, national, and international companies to support them. This support should be in donations as well as sponsorship.

Sir Claus Mozer and Karen Gadd.

c. The media must be brought in to credit arts sponsors as much as sports sponsors. For this to happen the arts must lose its ambivalence to sponsorship.

Sponsorship is a Good Thing
It is prostitution of our culture. Before approaching it, decide what you want, and what you can and want to offer.

Approach Sponsorship Positively
There is an excellent publication, 'The Impact of Tax Incentives on Arts and Museum Fund Raising'. I'm sure you all know it, as it sets out the arguments for increases in tax incentives. According to its survey 87% of the organisations surveyed give priority to seeking sponsorship, spending time and money in its pursuit. **Yet it says**, 'They expressed reservations about sponsorship including a belief that it is:

(i) A cheap form of advertising;

(ii) An attraction to safe products produced by prestigious arts organisations;

(iii) Easier in London.'

I will deal with all these in due course. What concerned me was the muddled thinking and approaches to sponsorship. Don't give sponsorship a priority in your organisation if you don't like it. If you don't like sponsorship you will meet with a limited response. It's no good regarding it as a necessary evil, it will muck up all your fundraising.

I am successful at raising sponsorship because I believe in it. I am astonished at the ambivalence towards it from those in arts funding. I went to an ABSA seminar which was introduced by their director Colin Tweedy who said 'let's assume that sponsorship is a good thing and not debate the principle of sponsorship.' This was said to a hall full of sponsorship managers and immediately gave the impression that even ABSA is not convinced by sponsorship. All of us in the hall believed in it enough to be devoting our energies to it. It comes as a shock that the only government funded body for sponsorship does not understand its position. It doubts the one activity it exists to promote, which may explain its inability to lead public opinion on sponsorship, and do nothing to lobby the press.

What hope for the rest of us!

The Positive Aspects
Sponsorship provides the funds and motivation to apply good management practice. This includes brilliant marketing, a sure way to attract and keep sponsors. Sponsorship allows **Music at Oxford** to produce superb literature for our leaflets, programme books, posters, etc. It has to be a high quality to justify the sponsorship; without the sponsorship we could not produce beautiful programme books.

Sponsorship is a serious part of our funding **and** it helps our planning. Sponsors will commit for three-year periods, they will confirm well in advance. Compared to public funding authorities in England sponsors are heaven to work with.

Stephen Mayes.

Sponsors' interval reception held in the Divinity School, Bodleian Library.

I believe sponsorship has an important role in arts funding, it is a very important part of the equation. **It does not replace Government Funding**, it complements it. I am not able to offer you any wisdom on Government funding. My personal belief, for what it's worth, is that without substantial government funding all of us and future generations will suffer. The Arts and our heritage must be a priority, and we are disgracefully underfunded at present. The present debates on percentage increases miss the main argument that it should be a tenfold increase not 10%.

One of the remedies we can apply is sponsorship. In **Music at Oxford** our funding is as follows:

Ticket Income	65%
Sponsorship	30%
Friends	2.0%
Grants	0.5%
Conference Management	2.5%

I don't recommend this as a model, far from it. A model for **Music at Oxford would be**

Ticket Income	55%
Sponsorship	25%
Friends	5%
Grants	15%

I would look for £100,000 in grants:

County Council	£25,000
City Council	£25,000
Arts Council	£50,000

All modest sums to finance 150 events a year. I would see the City and County money used to provide ticket subsidies, children's and youth events, and local music making; the Arts Council for new and adventurous music, ambitious concerts, etc.

Sponsorship would be used primarily for the safe events.

a. No form filling, give them a proposal. If they say yes (in writing), that is the money guaranteed.

b. Sponsors want you to succeed. If you sell out and achieve all you wanted they are delighted. (For public funding the motto seems to be **Don't be too successful**).

c. Sponsors care about the organisations they support, and will offer other help when you meet problems, or give you computers, or train your staff etc.

I know a lot of you will now be turning over in your mind dozens of horror stories about sponsors. I'm not saying that all sponsors are wonderful. But most of them tend to be a very positive influence on the organisations they support.

When you have good sponsors you like and trust, bring them onto your management, board etc. to help find more sponsorship. Despite our public school system we've still managed to produce some excellent managers. Sponsors who care about the arts are likely to be invaluable with your management and planning.

Sponsorship is not Fundraising
What is your organisation's funding portfolio? Where does sponsorship fit?

Events loved by sponsors are also loved by audiences and should not be neglected or diminished.

As it is I cannot ignore the immediate wishes of my audiences and sponsors. Consequently I am unable to develop the exciting areas of new music, unfamiliar music etc. except when subsidised by the Contemporary Music Network.

This is not a paper on **Music at Oxford**. I am merely using these as illustrations. Without funding I have created something exciting and successful **but** if funding was available I could do so much more. Public money would be well spent in my hands but it will never come my way unless attitudes change.

Now I know that most of you have a completely different piechart, where ticket income probably does not feature. I am not here to tell you how big or small that sponsorship slice should be for you. I would suggest it is as big as you can make without any compromise on your part. This does not mean you should not be flexible or make changes to accommodate sponsorship. If by spending an extra £20,000 on marketing and PR you can sell £100,000 of sponsorship then consider it.

When **Music at Oxford** started, the marketing was (and is) effective. This is expensive but worthwhile. It means I have a great deal to offer sponsors, they share the advertising value. Many people hated the pushiness of our publicity and said 'We don't do it like that in the Arts'. Why not?

Southern Arts gave as a reason (Excuse no. 789) for not funding us that we spend too much on publicity. 'Nobody else spends that much' they said. 'No one else sells out 90% of their concerts', we replied. The fact that we earn in ticket income many times what we spend on marketing is no argument apparently.

Sponsors love our good publicity. They share it very subtly, they never intrude on a concert, except to be

Presentation of sponsorship cheque. Ronnie Gorlin (Arthur Andersen), Karen Gadd, John Patten MP.

there as honoured guests. I do not tailor events to suit sponsors.

Don't Undersell Your Organisation

Getting the price right is essential for good sponsorship on both sides.

It is very hard to price sponsorship. I base my pricing on what I need to make each event happen, plus whatever I think I can get. Decide in what league you're in, and accept that you'll be undercut, accept that there may be others who get more, but be positive about what you are asking for.

If you believe the sponsor is getting too much for what he's paying, it will wreck your relationship. All I can advise is spy on all other similar groups and see what they are asking for. If you are uncertain you'll very quickly get a feel for what is the market range.

Also if you ask for too little, your sponsor will be worried! Most sponsors don't really appreciate bargains except occasionally. They think there's something wrong with your organisation.

Always listen hard before you name a price! The sponsor may have a budget beyond your wildest dreams. If possible establish the sponsor's ballpark on price before naming yours.

Sponsorship

Who should raise it? Raising sponsorship is a professional hard sell, it cannot be farmed out to well meaning committees of fierce ladies, or anoraked enthusiasts. It is important to be business-like, and to blend in with their method. If your image jars with the sponsor they will be uneasy.

Train as salesmen. There are many excellent one-evening courses on selling. Repulsive as the idea may sound **try one**. I did and next morning secured a £100,000 sponsorship, well worth the £60 for the evening course.

Know the techniques. There are several techniques for closing a sale which are very relevant to securing sponsorship. It is important to recognise a real buying signal, and to be able to distinguish it from someone being encouraging just to get you out of their office. It saves you huge disappointment later. Use the techniques very subtly or you'll compromise your credibility.

Prepare Your Literature

When offering sponsorship to companies show them samples of the sort of coverage they will receive. Also, have a clear plan of what you are seeking from the sponsorship and what you are offering in return. If possible, have a sponsorship brochure which sets this out. This need not be very glossy and expensive, it just needs to be clear.

Know Your Sponsors

When approaching a sponsor find out about their company and if possible their sponsorship policy and history. This will enable you to ask the right questions in your meeting. By asking questions you can maintain control. Listen intently to what the sponsor is saying and adapt what you are offering accordingly. If you cannot adapt to their needs, tell them and explain what you are offering them anyway.

Sponsorship meetings are rare and hard to establish, never waste one.

Understand the relationship. The sponsor is your treasured customer and should be treated very gently. Snivelling servility is as inappropriate as treating sponsors like street-wise spivs. It is a business relationship on both sides, you are selling a very valuable service to your sponsor, which has many elements including credibility in the community. This does not however give you any special rights over the sponsor. I remember one charity telling me how much they disliked sponsorship as the sponsor never seemed to be grateful enough. Gratitude has no place in this relationship.

Know when you have made a sale and when you haven't. Many companies like the idea of sponsorship but have inadequate budgets to fulfil all their wishes. Always get the commitment in writing, and do not assume that you have the sponsorship until then. I believe that most of the 'sponsor dropped out stories' are not true. Many of them are a result of wishful thinking and rather unbusiness-like practices.

What can You hope for in Sponsorship

The medium term relationship is the best you can hope for, always be looking for new sponsors. Avoid dependency, complacency and resentment. Expect your success rate to be depressingly low, sponsorship is there to be found but it is very hard to finally secure. Don't feel discouraged, sponsorship may be elusive, depressing, exhausting, and at times unrewarding. In the long term if you approach it correctly it is worth it.

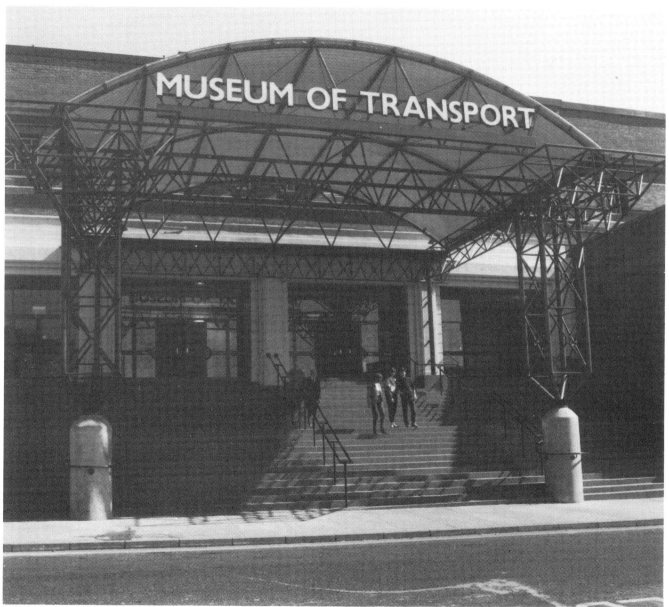

Main entrance to the Museum of Transport, Glasgow.

BUILDING AUDIENCES AND WINNING SUPPORT

Julian Spalding, Director, Glasgow Museums and Art Galleries since April 1989, was Director of Manchester City Art Galleries for four years. He is committed to public sector aid for the arts and to bringing the arts to a wider audience.

We have three million visits a year to our museums in Glasgow. We have tremendous public support, right across the social spectrum — every taxi driver I speak to thinks our museums are great (even when they don't know who I am) and tells me what's wrong with them (when they do). There's a real tradition of museum and gallery-going in Glasgow that survives from Victorian times, when we were one of the main forms of entertainment. This tradition has survived in Glasgow, partly because people live in flats and want something to do outside them, especially when it's raining, which it occasionally does. (One taxi-driver told me that the description of an intellectual in Glasgow was someone who went to Kelvingrove when it **wasn't** raining.) Above all, this tradition of gallery-going has survived because the District Council, which runs our museums, believes in them, and has put money into them, and has, above all, opened them and continued to respond to imaginative ideas about them, so they're kept in the public eye. What other local authority has managed to open a Burrell; then a new Transport Museum; and the first fully air-conditioned exhibition space capable of taking full-scale international shows outside London — The McLellan Galleries. Not all of that is the District Authority's money — some of it's from the Region and elsewhere, but without the District Authority's sums at the centre, not just the capital costs but the revenue

too, none of these projects would have happened. The commitment is impressive and the 1990 European Cultural Capital accolade well deserved.

But why all this, quite exceptional commitment? Why ever not, would be the right reply. We're talking about **Glasgow** — and that's the key, I think. Talking — museums in Glasgow get talked about a lot — the best marketing is by word of mouth. People in Glasgow talk about our museums and support us and it is that swell of public opinion that ultimately can be turned into cash. It's the use of public opinion that can unlock the coffers of both the public and the private sector — for both businessmen and politicians operate in the last analysis in the public arena — whether they're there for purchases or ideas — and we in museums operate in the public arena too.

I want to talk about our place in the public arena — about museums' role in a democracy and what that means and could mean. But, first of all I'd like, or rather I feel I ought, to make a confession.

I don't know anything about money. I don't understand it, if I'm honest, I don't think it exists. What is it? When you get close to it, it disappears — it's nothing but a rate of exchange. The deal done at a particular place and time, in particular circumstances between one person who has something he is prepared to sell and another person who wants it. Keep this in mind, that money is a hollow concept and it has no substance in itself, it's purely a way of describing a fleeting transaction between possession and desire, a shift sometimes of possessions, sometimes of power. It's an attempt to give concrete form to transactions that in many cases can't be quantified. What has this pound note to do with the delight people get at seeing, say, the paraphernalia of their youth? And yet, without it, it's difficult for them to get that experience. What has this note to do with appreciating a painting by Van Gogh? But you'd need more than this to do that now, especially if you'd want one of your own. Holding this pound note up makes me think of the Zen Buddhist who, surrounded by his pupils, pointed to the moon and told them all off for looking at his finger.

It is right to look at money — it's very interesting stuff — but it is only symbolic of what society chooses to evaluate in a certain way and in our society a lot of transactions are not evaluated in financial terms, like visits to museums — or they haven't been so far — and attempts to do so can restrict those transactions by emphasizing what is most easily quantifiable about them. I'll give you an example. When I came to Glasgow, I was immediately faced with the problem of whether to give the go-ahead to a project for a new natural history gallery which had a major sponsor wanting to put substantial sums into it, though the cost would have to be topped up by the District Council. Great. But when I looked at the designs, I discovered they were designed to cater for a maximum visitor throughput of four minutes per gallery. The scheme was originally conceived as a charging display and the cost-effectiveness depended on the numbers going through and the scheme was designed to channel them through at a certain speed, though not on a train like at Jorvik. For the cost of the whole display I wanted a more multidimensional experience — I wanted people to be able to linger and to explore things for themselves. The bottom line —

marketing plan, cost-benefit analysis — whatever you like to call it, had squeezed the substance out of this display. So I said no with the risk of losing the sponsor.

The quality of visit, the museum experience is what we should be addressing and where the really exciting challenges lie, whereas the cost-effectiveness approach has tended to encourage us to emphasise the immediate attractions at the expense of long term benefits. I'm all for interactive displays but they've got to lead somewhere. I took my son to the new insect gallery at the Natural History Museum — he's six. He darted about trying everything but when he'd made it work — I mean the machine work or when he'd done the computer game — he lost interest in it. What did he learn? I'm sure something, but there was no time or opportunity to develop that knowledge and really experience and understand it. Some of the games were, I thought, quite pointless. He discovered, having watched the lad in the queue before him, what part of the interactive video screen to press to build a correct model of an arachnid but what is the point of knowing what an arachnid is? I don't want to sound too critical for, as my colleagues in Glasgow know, I'm dead keen on interactive displays (we have virtually none and what we did have went a decade ago) but we have to do a lot with them and some of them are a con.

I took my son, too, to the new Design Museum — his only interest there was the interactive computer game called 'How to design a toothbrush'. So we sat side by side, each with our own video monitor, and listened to the client instructing the designer (that was us) as to her requirements for a new toothbrush — the cost — the time we'd got — the market — it was for young people who prefer transparent handles, we were told. Nothing was mentioned, by the way, about hygiene or mouth size or ecology. Nevertheless, on we went. My son's toothbrush ended looking short and dumpy like him, mine — well I disobeyed every client instruction — opted for an opaque handle and made it with a lump in the neck. To my delight and surprise, the client

Art Gallery and Museum, Kelvingrove, from Sauchiehall Street, Glasgow.

reappeared on the screen when we had both finished and told me how delighted she was with my design; and my son got the same message too. Well what do you learn from that? In a design museum, too! But, nevertheless, the computer tables were full. The same was true at the Natural History Museum, the insect gallery was packed, yet it had, I would guess, about two dozen real specimens in it — whereas a room upstairs, lined with geological cases packed with hundreds of specimens, was empty — save for two attendants. So we can't, as Sir David Wilson has written, be just about objects — we're about people too and we've got to bring the two together in a more rewarding way — that is the immediate challenge for the museums.

And I still call them museums and galleries not just because I can't think of better names. I thing our challenge is to make **museums** and **galleries** great places to visit — as many of them are — to make the public perception of them change. A friend of mine overheard a comment in a museum, one chap complaining to another, 'nothing changes in this place'. 'Don't be stupid,' came back the reply, 'it can't change, it's a museum.' Both have their point but if we concentrate only on one or the other, we'll lose our audience.

The recent political emphasis on shopkeeping has tempted many of us to develop the 'everything must go' sort of attitude to our displays — flashy and distinctly down-market — popular capitalism. There are several pluses to this and we will have drawn in a wider audience. But people get tired of perpetual sales and it is arrogant to think that we need not provide the best for everyone.

In the same climate many museums and galleries have decided to concentrate their resources on providing the best for the few. The educated scholar or the rich

The Hornby Portal at the Burrell Collection, Glasgow.

patron and their friends have been under threat from this new populism but have managed to survive and could well develop a new breed of exclusive museums (of which there are many in the States) under cover of the imposition of charges. I don't know about you but when I go to the V & A now, for all its cries of populism, I get the feeling of exclusiveness, of rich man's art. It may have been infuriatingly chaotic before but it was friendly and fabulous. Now, it's like an exclusive Knightsbridge store and the people are there to match. It smells now of wealth.

I well remember a comment from one of my councillors in Manchester who said that, 'you, museum professionals, when you go into a museum look at the displays; we, politicians, look at the people'. I make a conscious point now of doing both.

There is no question that the better off benefit more from our services — even in Glasgow where the majority of our resources are within easy reach of the residences of the rich. Charging must shift museum audiences more in this direction — to serve the better off rather than the poor. Though I've seen no statistics to prove it, that must be what's happened in London — the museums that now charge have shifted their audience base the social spectrum. The money they've made has resulted in the people with money benefiting more. The statistics prove that — the state subsidy per visit is higher in a charging museum than in a free museum. So money, as the old saying goes, attracts money. And it attracts sponsorship.

It used to be feared that the advent of sponsorship would encourage the arts to promote what was popular rather than the more difficult or esoteric. This has happened up to a point, but actually it's not what is popular that's being promoted so much as what is up-market. Those sponsors who have been attracted to museums have been those who have been interested most in the majority of our audiences, which are the educated middle classes with a particular brand of spending power. Karen Gadd's remark is a case in point — she can fill her concerts by putting her prices up. Museums and galleries may now be in the market place but they're in the up-market place. Roy Strong saw the two eliding so comfortably that he could conceive the V & A being the Laura Ashley of the 1990s.

Negotiating recently for a new line on products for Glasgow Museums, we wanted to reuse some of the fabulous designs of the Turkey Red Company — I'd like these to become something of a corporate image — an alternative to all that Mackintosh or Mockintosh — and for that we needed a name — not Turkey Red — but what about Glasgow Red? The business we are negotiating with was worried there may be some sales resistance, they said, to the political implication. I wonder if it'd been the same if the Turkey's were blue. They preferred, instead, the name the Glasgow Collection. Collection they assured us, like portfolio, had now all the right associations. I don't know what it is about capitalism but it seems to have an instinctive swing to the right.

Money attracts money, and we must all — even ourselves in Glasgow — note with envy Sir David Wilson's mention of the £3 million got every year in sponsorship for the British Museum.

The same feelings will undoubtedly be aroused in many of you in smaller museums than us when I say that so far in Glasgow we have raised about £400,000 in sponsorship for our 1990 programme — and we certainly need it — and more and more beyond that. But I don't agree with Sir David Wilson that we should look to the public sector for our base funding — building and staff only — and raise the rest — for all our activities, redisplaying, exhibitions, outreach programmes — from outside as if they were luxuries — not state responsibilities. He may be able to find the money — we can do quite well — but what about the small museums? How are they going to fare, with nothing like the glamour of Bloomsbury Square or the Burrell on offer?

It is so shortsighted for Government, any government, to provide a basic provision and then not to spend any money enabling it to take advantage of the base expenditure and operate to full capacity. Proportionally, the money needed to do all that programme of events, exhibitions, lectures, outreach services that will make the museum a vital part of its community — the money needed for that is proportionally small in comparison to the basic costs of looking after the museum and just opening its doors to the public. On going to Manchester, I negotiated a 15% rise in the budget, a joint venture between the Arts Council and the City Council under the Glory of the Garden Scheme; their 15% increase in budget led directly to a 300% increase in visitor figures.

The Glory of the Garden was a strategy introduced by the current Government though diametrically at odds with their policy of squeezing local authority expenditure as a whole. They eventually caught up with this discrepancy and I ended my time in Manchester negotiating a 15% reduction in my budget. The Government may bleat that they've sustained or marginally improved public expenditure in the arts but they totally miss out the disastrous effect that this squeeze on local authorities is having on their provision of cultural services throughout the country. But this is a separate paper.

At least the services of our programme in Manchester meant that the politicians cut the Galleries with reluctance whereas they may have cut them with eagerness and I managed to persuade them to do some of it by increasing income, with the result that they agreed to spend £300,000 capital on a new restaurant and shop, so we did rather well out of it, in a way.

However we might not have been able to agree this if our attendance figures had been as low as they were when I came — under 100,000 a year.

Money had been spent on the galleries during my

predecessor's regime — they were rehung and regilded — and a huge purchase had just been made — £1.8 million for a Duccio of which the city contributed only £100,000 — a remarkable, and it proved never to be repeated, fund-raising achievement — in the press all the time — a day-by-day cliff hanger story. One couldn't have asked for better publicity. But the remarkable thing is that, having checked the attendance figures before and after the arrival of the picture, they showed no difference. Perhaps they helped prevent a decline, I don't know. I'm not arguing against money being spent on acquisitions — I believe we should go on growing and developing.

It's just a damn nuisance that one aspect of our collections — fine art — has ceased to be an object in its own right but become just a vehicle for investment.

What we're seeing in Van Gogh's Sun Flowers is not a work of art but a form of money: yellow earth turned to gold — worthless in his lifetime — now virtually priceless. And the market in which it was sold was not an art market but a financial market.

I learnt this lesson early in my career when I was at a sale in London. A painting reached a record price — a mere £150,000 in those days — much to my surprise the place broke into applause and everyone went up to congratulate the buyer. They should have been commiserating with him for having paid so much! But no, they were delighted he'd managed to get the financial backing to pay so much, therefore raising the whole market in that area and more money all round for everyone who'd got them or sold them. What are museums doing in that game! Give me the French system — where the state takes priority over the individual. Whenever a public museum there wants to buy something at an auction it does not bid, but waits till the bidding stops. Then as the hammer falls, it stands up and says, that's mine, thank you very much.

But the recent heavy investment in art is changing museums in many other ways. Not just in the fact that it has seized up the movement of works of art and reduced exhibitions but it has encouraged museums to look to their assets, to sell. The current idea now in art museums in America and in Germany is that you buy art with art — and since art is now a form of money, there's a lot of power in this argument. If you don't, you miss out. How can we, in Glasgow buy a Picasso — and yet it could be a great and popular addition to our collections and the people of Glasgow have a right to see something by one of the great artists of our age.

But I'm totally against selling. My main reason is that it weakens our overall bargaining position. It not only puts off benefactors who may wish to give their collections to the museum — and it's immortality they're after — and if we show we're not immortal, well, they'll go elsewhere. Selling also reduces our power to interest our public because what we sell, if it's of any value, will be of value because it is at that moment highly prized by our society and people want to see it — we should be enhancing interest not exchanging it. And if we sell what we're not interested in, we won't get much for it and will quite probably cripple the interest of a future generation who, perverse as the young are will probably love what we hate. And lastly, if we sell, we reduce our bargaining power with the Government or any other funding body who will just say to us, if you want more money, sell some more.

Money is all about bargaining power — and our job is to increase that bargaining power so that we can improve our services. In many ways, we do not realise what bargaining power we have — which we can exploit more. First, there is our permanence. Then, and most importantly, there is our public role, our very effectiveness as an institution, our public support. This is not just of interest to sponsors but above all to politicians — and this is what we have to seek to develop — by building audiences and winning support. And for that we need steady and planned growth.

A regular increase in funding which will enable us to

The People's Palace, Glasgow.

plan and organise change — and we do need to change if we're going to keep our Museums and Gallery services in touch with our public. And, moreover, there is so much we haven't done, so many people we never reach.

There is so much to do, there is so much that our services can do to increase the quality of life of people who live in our areas and within reach of our Museums. To change with society and to reach out into areas not tackled before, we need development funds and we need the opportunity to experiment so that we can prove the efficacy of our case.

I have no hesitation whatsoever in asking for a regular and sustained increase in **public expenditure** on Museums and Galleries. Our society should be spending more on services such as ours that not only enable people to enjoy themselves but to learn as well. With us they can learn about the past, about the present and about things to come. Our services are moreover ecologically friendly, which is more than can be said for a lot of public expenditure, and there is a growing appetite for what we have to offer, almost hunger for the things we preserve, as we destroy so much about us.

I have no compunction therefore for in asking for more money from the public purse and I think those leaders of our profession who argued in the '70s, like Sir Roy Strong and Neil Cossons, that the spending had to stop, that the Welfare State museums were over, did a great disservice to our museums and galleries by wilfully accepting restrictions in public spending.

It is, I think, hypocritical to say that on the one hand museums and galleries need more money and argue for that expenditure from the private sector and yet to say at the same time that the Government should not spend any more money on them.

Of course, one should argue for more expenditure from the public sector as well as from the private sector. One wants an all round growth not the lop-sided developments we've seen in recent years. And one wants growth too, not just in one's budgets but in one's constituency, in one's power base and this is what museums have been deprived of. This is the diminished legacy that such directors leave us when, instead of arguing for a fractionally better cut of public expenditure, they imposed charges on their visitors and therefore reduced the numbers who actually benefit from our service. This reduction in numbers quite simply

reduces our bargaining base because those in distributing public largesse can simply say that you only appeal to a small minority of the public and indeed to those who are already well educated and better off. Why should we be spending any more on your services?

The important role our museums and galleries have to play within Glasgow's society as a whole (not just among the cognoscenti but for everyone) will have been lost if, heaven forbid, charges were introduced in the museums in Glasgow. It would not be long, I think, before, the three million or so visits per year that we currently enjoy would spiral down and our services would become marginalised, there for the odd tourist or for families who had visitors to take out as a special treat. But our role, in the daily life of Glasgow, would have been diminished and Glasgow itself would be the poorer for it. But this is exactly what has happened in London. The V & A I believe is a shadow of its former self. Our galleries and museums have become more and more concerned with wealth rather than with poverty, with luxury rather than with work. Surely part of the impetus for this must be the desire on the part of curators to create environments conducive to sponsorship entertainments — exclusive receptions in exclusive surroundings where all signs of poverty including the public are kept discreetly out of the way.

It's the public perception of art galleries and museums that interests me and I think our main challenge is to build on that perception to establish a real power base within the community. If we can establish a real body of support within the public and show that it is well spread throughout all levels and communities within our society then we shall have a real bargaining power with the politicians.

And the true bargaining power of our collections is that they provide us with the basis to increase people's interest in our collections. And it's this concept I want to end on. Interest has almost become a debased word in our society. It means the amount of money you gain from an investment. However, there is another more universal form of interest which is when you get interested in something. And what is interesting about this interest is that when you become interested in something it can not only change your life — but change the life of others. We are not, as the Museums Association slogan would have it, 'open for business', but open for interest.

Printed in Scotland for HMSO by (25151)
Dd 287411 C8 3/91

 **HMSO**

HMSO publications are available from:

HMSO Bookshops

71 Lothian Road, Edinburgh, EH3 9AZ   031-228 4181
49 High Holborn, London, WC1V 6HB   071-873 0011 (Counter service only)
258 Broad Street, Birmingham, B1 2HE   021-643 3740
Southey House, 33 Wine Street, Bristol BS1 2BQ   (0272) 264306
9-21 Princess Street, Manchester, M60 8AS   061-834 7201
80 Chichester Street, Belfast BT1 4JY   (0232) 238451

HMSO Publications Centre

(Mail and telephone orders only)
PO Box 276, London, SW8 5DT
Telephone orders 071-873 9090
General enquiries 071-873 0011
(queuing system in operation for both numbers)

HMSO's Accredited Agents
(see Yellow Pages)

And through good booksellers